# ADVANCE PRAISE FOR
# THE PURPOSE IS PROFIT

"*The Purpose Is Profit* provides the roadmap and motivation needed to win the startup game. It is required reading for every entrepreneur committed to building a profitable business."

> —**Barbara Corcoran,** *Shark Tank* Investor and
> Founder, The Corcoran Group

"There are no shortcuts. Startup success requires a solid business model, disciplined execution, and a profound commitment. *The Purpose Is Profit* provides blueprints and tools entrepreneurs need to start and scale a business."

> —**Joel Peterson,** Chairman, jetBlue Airways and
> Consulting Professor, Stanford Business School

"Unlike so many books on entrepreneurship, *The Purpose Is Profit* gets at the nub of what it takes to build a successful business. Ed talks the talk, and walks the walk, about the importance of factoring profit into every business decision."

> —**Larry King,** Worldwide Television and Radio Host

"*The Purpose Is Profit* provides the formula for scaling a business from startup to Inc. 500 and takes you into the board room for the sale to a Fortune 100. The book shares the inside story and the hard lessons every entrepreneur needs to know, covering both failure and success."

> —**Bill Teuber,** Vice Chairman, EMC Corporation

"Ed's book isn't just about profit—it's about following your inner voice and your destiny. It's about succeeding through integrity and giving back. It will put you on the path to responsible prosperity."

—**Rohan Marley,** Chairman, Marley Coffee

"This is an excellent book. *The Purpose Is Profit* powerfully describes the principles profitable businesses must follow and how failure to adhere to every one of those principles takes a business owner over that fine line into unprofitability. The book is exceptionally practical and candid, since, alongside his success story, one of the authors freely describes what caused his other start-up business to fail."

—**Michael Critelli,** Entrepreneur and former Chairman & CEO, Pitney Bowes

"*The Purpose Is Profit* will resonate with anyone who wants to start their own business. Each chapter puts you inside the startup machine—challenging you to turn the levers and gears to your own advantage. Anyone who wants to mitigate the startup risk should read this book."

—**Don Froude,** former President, The Personal Advisors Group of Ameriprise Financial

"*The Purpose Is Profit* is both entertaining and educational. It is like getting an MBA in entrepreneurship in 300 pages. This is a must-read book for any aspiring entrepreneur."

—**Maggie Wilderotter,** Chairman & CEO, The Grand Reserve Inn

"*The Purpose Is Profit* is a powerful guide for entrepreneurs at any stage. It combines the inside story with the tools you need to build a profitable business. I'll be encouraging everyone with a startup dream to read this book."

—**John "Randy" MacDonald,** former COO & CFO, TD Ameritrade

"I run an entrepreneurially driven group within a large organization and have asked our team to read the book and share five key take-aways they will use to transform our business. I am betting on a 5% increase in year-over-year growth across my team from implementing the advice in *The Purpose Is Profit*."

—**Pamela Newman,** President & CEO,
The Newman Group, Aon Risk Solutions

"As the first customer to introduce corporate real estate outsourcing while I was at Baxter Healthcare, it was obvious Ed and I were creating something new and disruptive. We were constantly learning and adapting to make this breakthrough idea work. *The Purpose Is Profit* captures the energy, the work ethic, and the persistence every entrepreneur needs to create and build a successful new venture."

—**Bill Agnello,** former SVP & Executive Officer,
Workplace Resources at Sun Microsystems

"*The Purpose Is Profit* is a very accessible account of what it takes to be a successful entrepreneur, and—importantly—what it takes to fail successfully. Learning from the personal accounts in this book, an aspiring entrepreneur can well understand the nature of the journey (s)he is embarked upon. I highly recommend it."

—**Polly Black,** Professor of Practice, Business and
Entrepreneurship, Wake Forest University

"*The Purpose Is Profit* is direct and honest. It makes no excuses about the hard knocks you'll face in building your own business. The book puts you in the shoes of the entrepreneur, conveying the good, the bad, and the ugly of what it takes to scale your own business."

—**Mykalai Kontilai,** Founder, Collectors Café
and former owner, *Nightly Business Rep*

"If experience is the best teacher, then *The Purpose Is Profit* is your best bet to learn from Ed McLaughlin, who has been there and done that, how to start and build a successful company from the ground up."

—**Henry DePhillips,** MD, FAAFP, Chief Medical Officer, Teladoc, Inc.

"Building a business is one of the most rewarding yet challenging experiences of a lifetime. If you are planning to start a business, why not mitigate your risk by reading *The Purpose Is Profit*? No one can promise instant success, but following the proven roadmap in this book will substantially increase your probability of startup success."

—**Bill Scheller,** President & CEO, BlackHawk Industrial

"*The Purpose Is Profit* takes the contrarian view on growth at any cost. Through a well-written and engaging narrative, it highlights the advantages of focusing on the fundamental but sometimes forgotten business principles of customer service, team building, sales, and profitable growth versus pursuing exponential growth at the risk of losing control. These are worthy considerations for every entrepreneur, particularly in the face of a changing investment environment."

—**Vincent Ponzo,** Senior Director, Eugene Lang
Entrepreneurship Center, Columbia Business School

*The* TRUTH ABOUT
STARTING *and* BUILDING
YOUR OWN BUSINESS

# THE

# PURPOSE

## IS

# PROFIT

ED "SKIP" McLAUGHLIN

## WYN LYDECKER

PAUL McLAUGHLIN

BLUE
SUNSETS
BOOKS

Blue Sunsets Books, an imprint of Blue Sunsets LLC
Darien, Connecticut
www.BlueSunsets.com

Distributed by Blue Sunsets LLC

*The Purpose Is Profit: The Truth about Starting and Building Your Own Business* is available at special discounts for bulk purchases. Special editions, including personalized covers, excerpts of existing books, or books with corporate logos, can be created in large quantities for special needs. For more information, contact Blue Sunsets Books at info@ThePurposeIsProfit.com.

Design and composition by Greenleaf Book Group
Cover design by Greenleaf Book Group

Cataloging-in-Publication data is available.

Print ISBN: 978-0-9863043-4-7

eBook ISBN: 978-1-62634-291-0

Printed in the United States of America on acid-free paper

First Paperback Edition

# DEDICATION

This book is dedicated to my wife, Barbara. As my life partner, Barbara provided unwavering support in the face of endless hours poured into an entrepreneurial venture with an uncertain outcome. Having grown up on a farm in Arkansas, Barbara understood the value of hard work and never questioned the time and sacrifice it took to build a successful business.

# CONTENTS

The pull is the overwhelming desire to realize your own business vision, to be in charge of your own destiny, whereas the push is the crystallizing moment when your need to start your business becomes greater than the fear of venturing out on your own.

You will substantially increase your probability of startup success if you build a business in which you have distinctive competence. What special knowledge, exceptional talent, or unique skill can you bring to your business?

When starting a business you need to organize your thoughts, goals, strategies, and plans so that you can realize your business vision—all while dealing with the nonstop challenges of preparing to launch. I call this active process dynamic planning.

product, and offer a superior value proposition, but you need to invest in a professional sales force to ensure your success.

## APPENDIX A:
## THE STARTUP ROADMAP:
## 21 STEPS TO PROFITABILITY

*The Startup Roadmap* is a step-by-step guide designed to help you understand the mechanics of starting and running a profitable business. The steps fall into three categories: Proof, Profit, and Potential. First, you need to develop and prove your idea. Second, you have to figure out if you can make a profit. Third, you need to estimate the business's ultimate potential for success. This manual walks you through the entrepreneurial thought process—the same process I used for starting USI. Following the steps in *The Startup Roadmap* will improve your probability of success.

## APPENDIX B:
## THE STARTUP FUNDING GUIDE

Every entrepreneur wrestles with the need for startup funding. How do you determine how much capital you really need? What are the essentials of financial modeling and forecasting? What are the costs of capital—both equity and debt? How does valuation influence cost and control? What are the sources of startup funding? Increase your bargaining power by taking the mystery out of the startup funding process.

# PREFACE

Making the decision to start your own business can be a daunting proposition. After all, you are betting on your ability to turn your idea into a profitable business. Besides risking your time, money, and reputation, you will be forced to do things you've never done before—all with no guarantee of success.

Recognizing the enormity of this challenge, I decided to write a book that would demystify the startup process by sharing the practical realities of launching and building your own business. Rather than only teaching entrepreneurial success principles, I wanted to put the reader in my shoes as I faced the uncertainties and struggled to start up.

*The Purpose Is Profit* tells the complete story of my business from startup to exit. The vignettes and anecdotes are reinforced with the tools necessary to start a successful business. Given the complexity, I asked my friend, Wyn Lydecker, to join the writing team. Wyn's track record working with entrepreneurs, combined with her previous consulting work for my company, made her a natural fit for the book. Simultaneously, I asked my son, Paul, to bring the millennial perspective, combined with his recent business school experience, to the project.

With the team in place, we set out on a three-year journey of researching, writing, and listening to the concerns of entrepreneurs around the world—all while crafting *The Purpose Is Profit*. It is a book for the kind of people that aspire to build a business that solves a problem, creates jobs, and makes a sustainable profit from the get-go.

A few words about our title . . .

From time to time over the past three years, we received feedback about our title, *The Purpose Is Profit*. Some people thought it conveyed a message of personal enrichment at the expense of others. Since this was not our intent, we considered changing the title to accommodate the dissenters—but we always came back to our core belief that the purpose of every business is to make a profit, because profit is the fuel for growth, sustainability, and social impact.

We have written this book with one goal in mind: to improve your probability of startup success. We encourage you to apply the lessons in *The Purpose Is Profit* to take control, start up, and build a profitable business.

# INTRODUCTION

People told me I was crazy. "You are going to fail!"

I can't blame my colleagues for saying that. I was setting out to start not one but two real-estate-related businesses in the midst of the major 1991 commercial real estate slump, brought on by the sweeping failures of savings and loans across the country. But I just had to do it. My heart told me the restrictions of a large corporation posed greater risk to my well-being than the uncertainty of starting my own venture. As it turned out, one of my businesses did fail. But the other one took off, generating a profit in its fourth month. My partners and I never looked back.

My purpose in writing this book is to eliminate the mystery of becoming an entrepreneur by sharing my experience and the principles I've learned from both failure and success. You, too, can conquer the fears holding you captive, preventing you from starting your own business. I hope my story will motivate those of you who are asking, "Should I look for a job or create my own job? Should I stay in the confines of my corporate position, or should I start a business of my own? Do I have what it takes to blast through the obstacles and risk it all?"

I was on the fast track, working for some of America's best-managed corporations, including IBM, Hewlett-Packard, and Trammell Crow Company. Still, something was missing. I was selling their products and services when I really wanted to create and sell my own. I was hungry for independent success and control. I yearned to hold out my ideas for the world to validate. I know these sentiments are not unique.

I resolved not to go to my grave without first starting my own business. But I had questions. What type of business would it be? What would be my product? How would I make money? Who would be my customer? I thought up different business models and new ideas every week for years. But when was it going to happen? I finally documented my commitment to start my own business by writing out a promise to myself, signing it in front of a witness, and carrying it in my wallet for years. I knew if I wrote down my desire as a covenant, I would make it happen.

Even while rising through the ranks of some of the nation's most respected corporations, I was growing tired of being told what to do, when to do it, and how to do it—especially when I knew there was a better way. Conforming to individual decisions driven by politics and having others decide where I fit in the pay-grade hierarchy was not my idea of the best way to make a living. Would my life just go on and on, tied to an income stream driven by the motivations of others? No. I wanted to take control of the mission for my life.

This book is all about that alternative path. If you do not like the choice of working for BigCo, then start NewCo. You will set the pace, the tone, and the direction. You will make the decisions, and you will be responsible for the outcomes. Yes, there is the risk of failure—but that is precisely why I have written this book. If you can understand the levers and gears within the startup machine, you can dramatically increase your probability of success.

Rather than a textbook approach, I want to share my startup experience by telling you the story of my journey, enumerating the principles of success and the hard lessons learned along the way.

I bootstrapped two companies at the same time. One startup was a passion project filled with promise that ended in commercial failure. The other startup not only thrived, it became an Inc. 500 Company and went on to be sold to a Fortune 100 Company. I want you to learn from both of these stories.

The essential difference between the two businesses was my distinctive competence. Distinctive competence is an exceptional skill or talent, specialized knowledge, and a record of achievement you've acquired through your unique experience. Having distinctive competence is Lesson #1: A venture filled with passion is not enough; you will substantially increase your probability of startup success if you build a business that leverages your distinctive competence.

———

Let me set the stage for my liftoff as an entrepreneur. It was 1990. I was 36 years old, married with two young children, and working for Trammell Crow Company (TCC), the largest US real estate developer. Trammell Crow paid me a good salary, but the industry was in turmoil. The traditional real estate development side of TCC was struggling for survival, and heads were starting to roll. On the other hand, our new service business was making money. Since the development side controlled the service side, there was tremendous political and performance pressure within TCC. This created trust issues around career, compensation, and control. My solution to this problem was always the same: outperform my goals.

By the summer of 1990, I became the top producer for the service business by landing what was lauded as the mother lode within the commercial real estate industry. It was the first comprehensive outsourcing contract for all corporate real estate service lines for a Fortune 100 company called Baxter International.

Even though it was a time to celebrate the Baxter victory, economic and internal political pressures were bearing down. TCC wanted to change my compensation package. Under duress, I agreed to accept a cut in compensation, with the understanding that I would be promoted to partner. My boss toasted my promotion with champagne at the holiday party in December—but the other shoe was about to drop.

Fast-forward three months to one fateful Saturday morning in March of 1991. I had been out of town all week, so I went into the office that weekend to clean up some paperwork. When I walked into the copy room, a spreadsheet sat on top of the copy machine. Not meant for my eyes, it outlined three go-forward scenarios for our business unit. Two of the three scenarios had me cut from staff.

That defining moment pushed me with two hands to take the leap to start my own business. It was the best decision I ever made.

———

Every entrepreneur faces the moment of truth. Clearly the tipping point for me was that fateful day in the copy room. When is the right time for you to start up? What kind of business are you going to start? And what are you going to do about it?

If you have the dream to become an entrepreneur and start your own business, this book was written for you. *The Purpose Is Profit* gives you the inside story from the entrepreneur's perspective. It covers the full arc—from the struggle to conceive the right idea, to funding the startup, to scaling the business, to executing the strategy behind the exit. Finally, the book discusses life after the sale to a Fortune 100 company—the good, the bad, and the ugly.

*The Purpose Is Profit* delivers direct insight about the startup process and how business really works. Each chapter tells a part of the story interwoven with the tools you need to build your own business. As a special feature, the appendix includes two essential manuals: *The Startup Roadmap* and *The Startup Funding Guide*.

It's your time. Take charge. Start up now.

As my late friend and mentor, John Stanger, entrepreneur and past head of General Electric Credit, said, "Do it! Do it! Do it!" I followed John's advice, and I think you should too.

SECTION

# 1

---

# PRELAUNCH

# 1

# THE PULL AND THE PUSH

People normally say "push and pull," but every entrepreneur I've known has first faced the pull, and then the push.

The pull is the overwhelming desire to realize your own business vision. It is a mind-set, a fire burning within you, and a relentless force like gravity. It is the knowledge deep within your soul that you will never be satisfied, and life will never feel complete, unless you start your own business.

The push is the crystallizing moment when your need to start your business becomes greater than the fear of venturing out on your own. It is the realization that you cannot work another day for someone else. Often, the push comes from an outside force that can literally shove you into becoming an entrepreneur.

For me, the final push was a long time coming.

I first felt the pull of entrepreneurship in 1976, the summer our nation celebrated its bicentennial. I was a teenage lifeguard on the

Jersey Shore. My days consisted of long spells sitting in the lifeguard chair watching people diving through the surf, playing on the sand, or swimming beyond the breakers.

While the public's safety was my main concern, sometimes, to keep my mind active, I thought up new business ideas.

Scientists had just begun to issue research reports warning that too much sun exposure caused aging, wrinkles, and skin cancer. Repeated deep sunburns were particularly dangerous. With zinc oxide streaked across my nose, I listened to these reports, and it hit me: Why not market a product to protect the skin from the sun's damaging rays? "Sunguard. From the People Who Know the Sun!"

My friend and fellow guard, Don Froude, and I got together every day after our shift and worked on the idea. When I told my father, he thought our concept was so good that he sent us to see his lawyer to get advice on how to proceed. My father made it clear that we had to pay the legal fees ourselves. That was okay with us.

*Ed and Don lifeguarding on the Jersey Shore*

It felt great to be taken seriously. We couldn't believe that we were meeting with a bona fide attorney. The lawyer set us up with a patent attorney who gave us an education about producing a skin lotion.

"You know, any time you develop a product that is going to go on your skin, you need to deal with the FDA. You need to test it to make sure it's safe. And you'll need to patent your formulation," the attorney said.

But somehow, we were not dismayed or overwhelmed. Don and I spent hours coming up with advertising ideas and even looking for a chemist until we headed off to college at summer's end. Although we never did start the business, our investment in Sunguard was time and money well spent. It educated us and lit the entrepreneurial fire, which was now burning within me, exerting its inexorable pull toward a goal of starting my own business.

## THE PULL CONTINUES

My college years at Holy Cross in Worcester, Massachusetts, reinforced the lessons of ethics and integrity my family had taught me. The breadth of a liberal arts education, combined with a sense of accountability and debate, challenged me to consider the ramifications of my decisions. While Holy Cross lacked a professional business program, it provided a framework for sound judgment and sensitivity to the needs of others that has stayed with me.

Without a business education, I tried to figure out how to launch my career. Every adult I asked, including some professors, advised me to get my MBA or go to work for a top corporation with a formal training program to learn about business.

I didn't waste any time. Even before graduation, I had lined up a job with IBM. In the late 1970s, IBM had the best training program of any company in the country. I was certain that IBM would provide me with the experience and knowledge I needed.

Two years at IBM not only taught me how to sell, but also about life in a huge corporation. Looking back, I now appreciate how fortunate I was to be introduced to the IBM Way. I learned how to develop a comprehensive value proposition and how to sell it to customers. In fact, IBM's sales techniques, discussed in detail in chapter 8, still serve me today.

But I also learned that I was not going to be happy in an environment that controlled almost everything about my life: how to dress, how your pay grade affects your status, which country club to join. I decided to leave for another technology firm, Hewlett-Packard (HP), because they had a more entrepreneurial reputation. HP, after all, had famously started in a Silicon Valley garage. And although the pull had a hold of me, I still felt the need to learn more about the world of business before starting my own venture.

The HP sales operation that hired me was located just outside Dallas, Texas, in a warehouse-like building, sitting out on the plains. HP was run by engineers more concerned about investing in new product innovation than spending money on a fancy office environment.

HP's business culture particularly appealed to me because it gave people enough rope to be innovative in their jobs. "Just don't hang yourself," my manager warned. Here was an environment where I could fit in and flourish.

My personal life also improved. Before long, I met and married Barbara Boyd. Barbara had recently graduated from Baylor Dental School in Dallas and started her own dental practice. Sure enough, she was living my dream, running her own business. Every night we discussed her business challenges and growth opportunities. Attracting new patients was the lifeblood of a new dental practice.

We spent hours talking about marketing programs that would rapidly build a clientele.

*Barbara Boyd, DDS*

Finally, the idea struck: *Gentle Dentistry* would become the theme for her marketing program (although this mantra is more common today, it was a breakthrough concept in the early 1980s). Barbara created a successful Gentle Dentistry direct-mail marketing campaign. Soon her practice was booming—until she received a cease and desist letter from the state dental board. You see, they didn't like the implication that Barbara's dentistry was gentle, while other dentists' were painful. Oh well, at least Barbara got the benefit of the Gentle Dentistry campaign while it lasted.

Although Barbara was open to my ideas and input, she started to realize that I was trying to relieve my new-business frustrations through her dental practice. Everything came to a head on our monthly drive to Arkansas to visit her folks. Can you imagine getting an earful of business development strategy for seven straight hours while trapped in a car? As soon as we left Dallas, I'd start in on all the ways she could improve her business, from back-office management to marketing to bringing in more patients.

Finally, on one of those long drives, Barbara turned to me and said, "You know, Ed, you really ought to start your own business." With a bit of sarcasm, she added, "You can take all that energy you have and put it into something of your own."

She was right. Instead of having the guts to start my own business, I was acting the part of an entrepreneur vicariously through her business. I'd wake up in the middle of the night thinking about how much I wanted to run my own show, to make my own decisions, and to live or die by them. I spent hours tossing around new business ideas—so much so that I became frustrated, anxious, and impatient. I was passionate about starting something, and Barbara was giving me the first of several small pushes. Yet I still lacked the confidence, the competence, and the big idea I knew were crucial for launching a successful business.

## THE PROMISE

Then one day when I was feeling particularly frustrated about my career, I had lunch with a trusted friend and respected advisor. Her name was Annette Field. Our conversation turned to my job and the plans I had for my future. Over the years, I had consulted with Annette on everything from my personal goals to purchasing Barbara's engagement ring.

She looked me straight in the eye. "Are you happy, Ed?" Annette asked. "Where do you want to go with your career? What are you doing about it?"

When I shared my desire to start my own business, Annette told me that one of her sons, who was my age, had left a big accounting firm to start his own practice. "He is very successful and truly happy—far happier than he ever was working for someone else."

The discussion hit a nerve. When we got back to her office, I asked Annette for a piece of paper, took out a pen, and wrote down a promise to myself that I would start a business within the next five years. Then I signed it and asked Annette to add her signature as my witness.

Once I had that paper in my wallet, I was finally able to sleep at night.

*The promise*

If you're feeling the pull toward the entrepreneurial life, sit down and craft a covenant. Document your goal to start up a business and sign it in front of a trusted friend. It can make all the difference. Although I did not formally launch my business until 1991, documenting my startup commitment resolved my internal conflict and memorialized my plans for startup.

My promise was in my pocket when I went into work at HP one Saturday. Coming out of the Texas heat, I entered our air-conditioned building and walked into our cavernous sales arena. As I looked across the sea of empty desks, a senior HP sales executive and mentor spotted me and came over.

"Ed, if you're going to work this hard," he said, "then you should be working for your own account. You'll only realize the real benefit of all your efforts that way."

I distinctly remember my response, "I'm dying to start my own business. I just don't know what kind of business it should be."

"You can make so much more money, have so much more control, and have so much more freedom in the long run," my mentor said.

Here, a man I respected had just validated my burning desire and given me yet another push. What was holding me back?

## THE PULL LEADS TO A NEW DIRECTION

As I wondered what sort of business I should start, I saw people in Texas reshaping the suburban landscape. Many of them were my peers. Previously, most large office buildings had been in central business districts, with the majority in downtowns. Now, office space was sprouting up all over, even in rural areas. I realized that I wanted to be part of that growing industry—commercial real estate.

An old friend, former HP colleague, and recent Harvard Business School graduate, Henry Johnson, had just joined Trammell Crow Company, the nation's largest real estate developer at that time. Trammell Crow had hired Henry in their Dallas headquarters to help start a new division called Trammell Crow National Marketing (TCNM). The division would sell and lease TCC's real estate directly to 30 designated accounts within the Fortune 500.

Traditionally, real estate firms were organized in local markets, waiting for corporations to come to them when they had a real estate need. Transactions happened only at the local level. But this new division would go out and ask for the order from the source at national headquarters.

Henry called me up and said, "You need to be part of this." He told me I could be a significant contributor in this new startup group.

The offer was irresistible. I said to myself, *I'm going for it!*

Now, I would be part of something small, new, and growing that would partly satisfy the entrepreneurial pull. As a sales executive with TCNM, I traveled to my assigned accounts in the Midwest to cultivate relationships with their corporate real estate departments. We set out to become the corporation's single point of contact for commercial real estate.

Trammell Crow National Marketing was highly competitive and focused on results. Their aggressive reward system fed these goals.

This entrepreneurial environment within a larger enterprise began to satisfy my hunger to create genuine value. Our small real estate services division started to add meaningful revenue and profit to Trammell Crow's bottom line. As we grew the business, we expanded into the lucrative Northeast Corridor, crowded with the headquarters of the majority of the Fortune 100 companies.

I relocated from Dallas to Stamford, Connecticut, and worked my way up and became the top rainmaker. After two years of dedicated work, I brought in the single largest real estate services deal ever completed. The contract comprised the complete and exclusive reengineering of Baxter Healthcare's distribution centers. That experience was exhilarating and kept my entrepreneurial fires stoked.

I had worked hand in hand with my customer, Bill Agnello, who was Baxter's Vice President of Real Estate, to develop a system that could manage the consolidation of all Baxter's distribution centers after the firm acquired American Hospital Supply. At that point, no other health-care supply company had more distribution space. We had to find a way to eliminate redundancies while expanding Baxter's distribution network.

To accomplish these goals, we utilized Baxter's business framework, which they labeled Value-Managed Relationships. This relationship structure connected Baxter and TCC around a common management system responsible for delivering hard savings, increased flexibility, consistent quality, and access to specialized resources with superior execution. Essentially, we reinvented the entire real estate delivery system for Baxter, which grew to include the comprehensive outsourcing of all real estate projects and personnel to Trammell Crow. As a result of the Baxter outsourcing contract, TCNM was rebranded Trammell Crow Corporate Services, and the division transitioned from being a marketing arm to a full-fledged profit center.

*Bill and Ed*

The Baxter deal woke me up. It clearly showed me that I could create a new way of doing business and deliver genuine value to corporations by serving their real estate and facilities management needs. This newfound knowledge made me realize that I had a distinctive competence that I could bank on to start my own business. As you will read in chapter 2, distinctive competence is a combination of unique skills, experience, and knowledge you have acquired over time.

This feeling of having a distinctive competence was exactly what I had been seeking. It made me realize that becoming an entrepreneur was now an achievable goal.

## THE PUSH

As a result of what we had accomplished with Baxter, Trammell Crow Corporate Services was no longer something small and entrepreneurial. Our division was delivering significant profits to the company's bottom line. The political pressure around compensation and control became a big issue and began to wear on me.

Concurrent with the explosive growth in corporate services, the real estate development business was in free fall. The incredible expansion in development that had initially excited me was turning into a massive oversupply. The nation's economy—and commercial real estate in particular—were in a downward spiral. These factors made the environment at Trammell Crow turn darker.

At the office, I sensed the need to keep looking over my shoulder, watching what I said, and feeling as though I needed to kowtow to the people above me. My productivity suffered because I felt I could not trust the system, and my heart was not in my work.

In the midst of all this, it became clear that our division's success had become the envy of the faltering development side. The services division had been subordinate to the larger, more profitable development business. Suddenly the roles were reversed. The service business was positioned to become the future of the company, which rankled the interests of some of the leadership. This shift in power created tremendous pressure within our group.

The tensions around compensation and control continued to mount. Even though Trammell Crow made me a partner, the promotion came at the cost of being forced to accept a reduction to my compensation. A few months later, when I found the spreadsheet in the copy room that showed scenarios cutting me from staff, it became clear that my efforts and approach were not valued by everyone in the hierarchy.

I was stunned. How could a newly minted partner, who had just landed the largest real estate outsourcing deal in history, be targeted for elimination? I felt blindsided and completely disillusioned. The whole incident stabbed at the heart of my loyalty. There was no turning back. This was the final big push.

My time had come. I was going to take control and start up. I was going to build a business where integrity, hard work, and creating value were rewarded more than playing politics. At the same time, I recognized my distinctive competence would enable me to be the architect of a new business model; figure out how all the pieces fit together; and create value for corporate clients. If the outsourcing value proposition had worked for Baxter, there was no reason that it would not work for many other corporations.

I began to plot my course to build a corporate real estate outsourcing business. At the same time, I conceived a second new business to address the oversupply of commercial real estate from the S&L crisis. It seemed every corporation and institution was flooded with surplus real estate. If I could help solve this vexing problem,

I felt I could meet my customers' greatest need, build a defensible business, and generate substantial profits.

My plan was to develop and produce a publication that included a compendium of surplus real estate for corporations and institutions to create a global market for buyers and sellers. Even though I became enamored with the idea of the publication, I had to acknowledge my lack of experience and expertise in the field. Given the scale and scope of this publishing venture, and knowing that my distinctive competence lay in developing and selling outsourcing services, I decided to focus on the outsourcing business first. Once the services business was established, I would start the publication as a second step. The publication became my passion project, the subject of chapter 7, "A Hard Lesson."

## ACKNOWLEDGE THE PULL, AND ACCEPT THE PUSH

Working for myself has been far more exciting and rewarding than anything else I have ever done. In the rest of this book, you'll see how I finally started my business and turned it into a multimillion-dollar enterprise. It all started with that promise in my pocket: *Own my own business by 10-5-88.*

Acknowledging the pull means becoming aware of an unserved need or an existing imperfection, coupled with a burning desire to do something about it. Accepting the push is more difficult than acknowledging the pull. The push is the realization that no matter how hard you work, how much you produce, and how much value you create, you cannot change the hierarchy, the politics, and the motivations of those who control your fate.

## THE PULL

- Are you dying to take control of your own destiny?

- Do you have a great idea for how to fill a real need?

- Do you believe your idea could transform lives for the better or disrupt the way business is done?

- Do you have a special talent that friends tell you to use to start a business?

- Do you have a unique competence in an area that you can use to create a business?

- Do you want to disrupt the status quo with a new product or service?

- Do you want to leave your mark on the world?

- Are you on fire to start your own business?

## THE PUSH

- Are you tired of working for someone else, being told what to do, and precisely how to do it?

- Have you lost your trust in "the system"?

- Does Human Resources make you feel like a replaceable part?

- Have you been waiting in line, answering ads, attending interviews, but never landing an actual job?

- Are you looking over your shoulder in fear at work?

- Have you had enough of playing the game by other people's rules?

- Are you dying to make your own rules and create your own business culture?

# 2

# DISTINCTIVE COMPETENCE

I struggled for years pondering the type of business to start, its potential for profit, and the cost of possible failure. I thought through hundreds of scenarios and the associated risks, constantly questioning the probability of success. One day, it struck me: The answer to my questions was distinctive competence.

The success of the Baxter outsourcing deal was the defining experience that made me realize I truly had a distinctive competence. As I looked back on all my past successes, I began to see a pattern. Each success relied on some unique skill, experience, or talent that set me apart.

All of my unique attributes came together to win the Baxter deal. I got very close to my customer, Bill Agnello, and truly understood Baxter's pain. I had an intimate knowledge of the real estate industry and the problems with the existing service model. With traditional barriers lifted, I had the freedom to innovate and address every significant pain point. I was highly competitive and comfortable challenging the status quo.

All this defined my distinctive competence. I now understood that if I built a new business around my distinctive competence, I could substantially improve my probability of success.

The same principle applies to you. If you can identify a need for a product or service in an industry where you have a distinctive competence, you could develop a bankable business idea. You could minimize the risks by utilizing your knowledge of customer needs, industry trends, operational requirements, financial models, relevant technologies, and potential competitors.

To discover and define your distinctive competence, ask yourself some questions:

- What special knowledge, talent, or skill do you have?
- Do you have a track record of success in a particular field?
- What unique experience or achievement can you apply to a new business?
- What additional competencies do you need to succeed?
- How can you fill the competency void?

Challenging yourself to answer these questions honestly and directly will fortify your startup and your long-term success.

After wrestling with these questions and reflecting on my past success, I realized my distinctive competence was my intimate knowledge of the value drivers behind real estate outsourcing. Since the Baxter deal was the first of its kind, the commercial potential to bring this model to market was phenomenal. Every corporation or institution with 100 or more locations was a candidate for outsourcing. The value proposition for the customer was undeniable, and the profit potential for my new business was huge. We were positioned to introduce a truly disruptive service model to the market.

## FUSION

While I was busy organizing my startup plans, word got around about the financial impact of the Baxter deal. So much so that the distribution industry association, Council of Logistics Management, invited Baxter and Trammell Crow leaders to present a case study of our partnership at their annual convention. Baxter's head of distribution and I were the primary speakers. We explained our innovative approach for driving savings while we engineered a new distribution network.

The discussion drew an overflow crowd, partly because our work had constituted the single largest real estate services deal done to date, and partly because many companies were consolidating their distribution centers in an effort to cut costs during the economic downturn.

Throughout the question-and-answer session, most of the queries were aimed at me. Soon I began to realize that members of the audience considered me the expert and that my distinctive competence had value in the marketplace.

I could draw on my experience to establish my new company. And since I had already put the details of the business case together for the Baxter deal, I felt confident that I could resell the value proposition to other corporations as a powerful alternative to the traditional model for managing corporate real estate.

After the panel discussion, there was a mob scene of distribution executives seeking additional insight and peppering me with questions: "How did you get the approval to single source?" "How do you measure the savings?" "How did you manage the disruption from outsourcing?"

One of the more inquisitive members of the audience was a man named Bill Scheller. Bill was the head of distribution at Patterson Dental, the largest distributor of dental equipment and supplies in the nation. He pulled me aside after the session, confiding that Patterson was about to consolidate their distribution centers and needed a company to manage the process. I was elated and agreed to a follow-up meeting.

Back at Trammell Crow, I suggested to my boss that we pursue the Patterson Dental opportunity, only to be met with resistance. My boss told me Patterson was too small for Trammell Crow.

I knew Patterson was not a Fortune 100 company, but it did represent solid business at a time when Trammell Crow's development business was turned on its head. TCC was losing partners every day, and morale was at historic lows. The service business was positioned for takeoff, but the economic meltdown of TCC's development business was thwarting the growth needs of the service business. And in the midst of all this corporate upheaval, I had come across the spreadsheets indicating that I might be cut from staff. Taken together, all these factors continued to propel me to leave TCC, pursue my new business, and change the course of my life.

I thought to myself, *Patterson Dental is not too small for me!*

## PROOF OF CONCEPT—PREORDERS

Now, I had the opportunity to give my business idea a head start. I took some vacation and got on a plane to Minneapolis, where Patterson Dental was headquartered. I knew this meeting would be a key test for my proposed venture. Could I bank on my distinctive competence? Even though I did not have the infrastructure, did I have the credibility to attract a significant first customer? I needed to find out before I quit my job for good. Thank goodness, I did not have a non-compete agreement.

At Patterson Dental, I told Bill that I was formulating plans to start my own real estate outsourcing business and would love to have his company as my first customer. I felt confident that I could help Bill reengineer Patterson's distribution network. It was the moment of truth. Was Bill Scheller willing to give a startup its first preorder?

Bill could not have been more encouraging. "If that's what you're going to do, sign me up."

While I was in Minneapolis, I went across town to visit one of my existing customers, Kip Chaffee, head of real estate at IDS Financial Services, which later became American Express Financial Advisors, and is now known as Ameriprise. They were in a high-rise, the very opposite of the plain brick, warehouse-like building that Patterson Dental occupied.

I had a very good relationship with Kip and felt I could trust him as an advisor and a friend. Plus, even though IDS was a Trammell Crow customer, my bosses weren't totally comfortable with its size. More and more, it seemed as though the middle to high-end market was wide open for new competitors.

When Kip heard what I was planning on doing, he did not hesitate to give his endorsement. After all, I knew the account, the work requirement, the people, and the way to get things done at IDS. Besides, Kip knew he could trust me and that I would not let him down. He enthusiastically confirmed that IDS business would go my way.

I returned to Connecticut elated. I couldn't believe that I had bagged two significant preorders in Minneapolis for a concept business in Connecticut.

My trip to Minneapolis gave me proof of concept. I had validation that real people in real companies believed the service I would be offering would solve a problem for them. *And* they were willing to place a preorder for real estate outsourcing services from me.

Securing preorders is a vital psychological and economic hurdle that every entrepreneur needs to clear. There is no reason to organize for mass production or service delivery without preorders in hand. I would not have started United Systems Integrators Corporation (USI) without the preorders from Patterson and IDS.

## APPLICATION

In retrospect, I realize that Bill Scheller, Kip Chaffee, and I were kindred spirits. We were uncomfortable with the status quo, open to new ways of doing business, and willing to take a calculated risk with people we respected.

Such relationships can only be cultivated when you have distinctive competence. My distinctive competence centered on my outsourcing value proposition, my track record of driving customer savings, and my industry relationships.

I believe that every successful business, big or small, is built on distinctive competence. The challenge is to determine your distinctive competence and apply it to a bankable business model that serves a customer need.

Identifying your distinctive competence will provide you with the following:

- The confidence to leave your job and start a new business
- The expertise to develop and execute a business model
- Access to a broad base of high-trust relationships
- Credibility with potential customers and suppliers

- Ability to attract a management team and secure financing

Even with distinctive competence, you should expect roadblocks. Soon after I started USI, I went to Chicago to pitch my old TCC customer at US Gypsum, a large building and construction company primarily known for producing wallboard. Even though I knew the head of corporate real estate, he politely listened to my startup story and then said, "We do serious business here. We don't have time for fledgling startups. You do not have the infrastructure needed to support our business. This meeting is over."

That experience opened my eyes and made me realize that the Fortune 100 did not make much sense as my primary target. Even though I had strong relationships with Fortune 100 firms, I needed to pivot and refocus my energy on the middle market and grow my business from there.

## COMPLEMENTARY RESOURCES

You can't do everything yourself. Getting preorders was one thing, but having spent my whole career working in teams, I knew I needed to find professionals with other competencies that would complement mine.

Fortuitously, my first answer came at an outdoor fund-raising event. Looking across the tent, I happened to spot an old high school friend, Maria LaMura, from New Jersey. I made my way through the crowd to say hello and catch up on old times. Then Maria introduced me to her husband, Ridgway Barker—Ridg for short—an attorney who worked at the top law firm of Kelly Drye & Warren.

Ridg and I warmed to each other immediately. I told him that I was planning to start my own business. "I'm dealing with a whole lot of unknowns. But I know I need a lawyer to advise me because I have never started a business before. It seems like a black box to me. I don't want to make a mistake," I said.

Ridg made me feel confident. "Good for you for pursuing your dream," he said. "I can help you through the process in getting started. It's a lot easier than you think. I have helped form many new businesses. Let's plan to meet in my office next week." He gave me his card and invited me to call him.

When we met at his office, Ridg put me completely at ease by asking fundamental questions about the business and taking the mystery out of the legal requirements for starting up. He wanted to know everything about my plans.

- What was my idea?
- Was I selling a product or service?
- Was I planning to grow (scale) the business to a much larger size?
- Would I have partners or employees?
- Who would be my customers?
- Where would I operate my business?
- Did I have intellectual property I would need to protect?
- Did I have a non-compete agreement?

He explained the importance of protecting my personal assets from liability by setting up a legal entity to house the business, a point we will cover in chapter 3. Ridg took me through other steps, like getting tax IDs. Then he gave me some basic legal forms, including non-compete and non-disclosure agreements, which he said would be essential as the business grew. Like any good attorney, he wanted to help me minimize risk.

"You don't want employees leaving and taking intellectual property with them. You don't want them opening up a competitive business across the street," he said.

And at the end of the hour, he said, "You can do this." My confidence soared.

## BUILDING THE TEAM

I had learned over the years that teams tend to create more value than individuals. I knew that trust was the key to finding the right people for my team. This was an important factor as I searched for people with competencies that would balance out and add strength to my own.

Naturally, the people I first approached were my colleagues at Trammell Crow. I knew these individuals from working together in the trenches, pulling all-nighters, and doing whatever was needed to win business. Additionally, since TCC hired from the best business schools in the country, my colleagues knew how to develop a business model and execute a plan. I thought I had a target-rich environment for sourcing my management team.

I put together a shortlist of TCC candidates. Given the turmoil at the company, I thought I could easily recruit a few team members. But everyone turned me down. It seemed that no one wanted to take the risk of leaving a regular salary and benefits to work for a startup, particularly in an economic downturn.

I had to rethink my recruiting plans and focus on what I really needed. Since I would be responsible for the business model, sales, and company strategy, I needed two teammates: one to execute the business and one to manage the back office. There were three main hiring criteria:

- They needed to be trustworthy.
- They needed to be team players.
- They needed to have a powerful work ethic.

Although it would have been nice, I really didn't need a Harvard MBA. We were not developing leading-edge technology. Initially, we would be conducting local market due diligence and negotiating real estate deals.

## My Partner, Gus

Sometime before I had decided to leave Trammell Crow, a recent college graduate named Gus Poulopoulos had sent me a letter saying he would do anything to get a job in commercial real estate. Gus was so determined to achieve his goal that he passed on other opportunities to gain a position in the industry. Since graduation from Fordham University, he was biding his time and paying his bills by working as a waiter. No wonder Gus truly understood the importance of providing superior service and tenacious follow-up. He kept calling me back and finding thoughtful ways to stay in front of me. "Just give me a chance," he said. I agreed to meet with him and wound up pitching my boss on giving Gus a try as a summer intern at Trammell Crow.

We assigned Gus to do a site search project in the local real estate market, and he did an excellent job despite working in the broiling summer heat. It seemed as though Gus would do anything to demonstrate his work ethic and competence. But when I recommended him for a full-time position, my boss said, "No, TCCS has no openings." I was frustrated with his response. Since Gus had fulfilled his commitments, I felt that we owed him the opportunity.

Now, as I searched for potential partners, I couldn't help but think of Gus. He was service-oriented, extremely diligent, and very trustworthy. Gus was a perfect fit to serve customers and execute the work. Besides, I just knew he would make a solid teammate. Gus jumped at the opportunity to join me.

## My Partner, Tom

You never know where you are going to find your partners. I needed someone I could really trust to run the back office. This would not be an easy position to fill, given my propensity to keep a tight grip on the numbers. One day it struck me. My TCC assistant's husband, Tom Dever, could be an excellent fit.

I'd gotten to know Tom because he picked up my assistant, Wendy, every day after work. We often chatted in the parking garage and became friends. Over the years, Barbara and I had Tom and Wendy over for dinners and even to celebrate holidays together. Tom was dependable, hard-working, and honest to a fault. If Tom made a commitment, you knew the job would get done.

Timing was good because Tom was looking for a position with ownership. I felt strongly that Tom would succeed in whatever he put his mind to, and I knew he would never let me down. I offered him a job with my new venture. Tom said, "I'm in."

*Tom, Ed, and Gus*

## CULTURE AND PRACTICE

Since I wanted to start a business built on a culture of trust and accountability, I wrote out exactly what my expectations were for Gus and Tom and laid out their compensation and benefits in detailed employment offers. I knew I couldn't afford to pay them much and instead offered each of them a five percent equity stake in the business. And since I was bootstrapping the business, I knew that I could not take a salary at all in the first year. I was focused on building revenues while minimizing expenses to get to breakeven as soon as possible.

Following Ridg's advice, the employment offers also included non-compete and non-disclosure agreements, which became USI's operating standard. In order to establish the foundation for USI's culture with its employees, the employment offers included the following language:

This employment offer is based on your commitment to USI's Standard Business Practices and Operating Philosophy including the following:

- Making commitments and keeping them
- Providing total quality and integrity in everything you do
- Being a team player
- Holding yourself accountable to the USI team
- Holding the USI team accountable to you

This exact language was used in all USI employment offers from then on. Gus and Tom were totally on board with everything in their agreements. These first documents set the tone and started the culture and practice I wanted to create around compensation, productivity, and morale. I believe that team members are better equipped to focus on bottom-line results when they have a crystal-clear understanding of their goals, responsibilities, and reward structure.

## DISTINCTIVE COMPETENCE IS THE KEY

Having identified the distinctive competence that would be the basis for our business, we had to figure out how to get the business off the ground. I was counting on my knowledge of real estate outsourcing to guide us as we developed the details of our business model, planned our rollout, and began to turn our preorders into a revenue stream.

Your distinctive competence should be the source of your new business idea. It is the one thing that will set you apart from your competitors and improve your probability of startup success.

# DOORWAY TO DYNAMIC PLANNING

When starting a business, you need to organize your goals, strategies, and plans to align with your business vision—all while dealing with the nonstop challenges of launching.

## DISTINCTIVE COMPETENCE

- Do you have a unique skill, special knowledge, experience, or talent?

- Does your skill or knowledge have value in the marketplace?

- Can you use your unique competence to create something disruptive, innovative, and valuable?

- Can you secure preorders to validate your concept?

- Do you have mentors and advisors whom you trust to provide constructive feedback?

- What professional guidance do you need?

- Have you identified a law firm to advise you?

- Do you have a plan to protect your intellectual property?

- What management resources do you need?

- Have you identified your management team?

- How will you reward your management team?

- Do you have a plan to document your management and employee agreements?

# 3

## DYNAMIC PLANNING

We were going to be a small upstart competing against established behemoths. The big real estate companies weren't paying attention to outsourcing, but we knew it wouldn't be too long before they would realize that it wasn't just a fad. We had the first-mover advantage, so we needed to pay attention to the clock, take action, plan, and organize all at the same time. I call this multitasking process *dynamic planning.*

Dynamic planning is the pursuit of your new business vision while dealing with a bevy of unknowns and maintaining a stranglehold on pre-startup expenses. A dynamic plan is an active plan—not a static, formal business plan. It is defined by your goals and continuously altered by new information. A dynamic plan creates a roadmap for developing a profitable new business.

*If you would like to get into the nuts and bolts of planning your startup right now, you can turn to* The Startup Roadmap *in appendix A.*

In many respects, the discipline of dynamic planning is the entrepreneur's dilemma. Most entrepreneurs are chomping at the bit to launch, accumulating expenses even before figuring out the mechanics of the business. Dynamic planning, on the other hand, challenges you to figure things out and address the unknowns prior to formal launch.

## USI'S DYNAMIC PLAN

I could not afford to fail. I had to plan the business, secure preorders, and resolve uncertainties before I quit my job. Except for a limited amount of pre-selling expense, I did not spend any money until my team and I had completed the dynamic planning process. We invested six months of our time in careful speculation prior to our formal liftoff—all without compensation. Dynamic planning was a key to our success at USI.

During the spring and summer of 1991, Gus, Tom, and I spent weekends gathered around my kitchen table. Barbara cleared the kids out, and we began documenting our goals and iterating the plans for building the business using flip charts and markers. When the summer heat became oppressive or my family needed the space, we escaped to the local library, where we locked ourselves for hours into a cramped but air-conditioned study carrel.

## BUSINESS VISION AND VALUES

The first questions we tackled were: *What was our vision, and what were our values?* Based on my recent experience, the answers were clear. We would build a real estate outsourcing business sensitive to the needs of our customers and our employees. We would deliver more than just superior service; we would provide our customers with a basket of integrated capabilities producing savings well in excess of cost. Our goal was to develop sustainable relationships built on a foundation of trust and integrity; creating loyalty so our customers would keep coming back for more. Everything we were setting out to achieve would flow from our vision and values.

## TARGET CUSTOMER

After we determined our vision and values, we defined our target customers and the benefits we would offer them. After meetings like the one I'd had at US Gypsum, we decided to target medium-size corporations in the Fortune 1000. This segment of the market was underserved since our competition was focused on the largest companies in the Fortune 100.

Having settled on the mid-level segment, we decided to pursue the heads of finance, distribution, and corporate real estate as our ideal customers. They were the ones who could understand the value of our services, and they were the ones with the purchasing authority. Getting our target customers defined so clearly enabled us to focus our efforts and not waste time or money chasing the wrong players.

Armed with a clear vision of our target customers, we were ready to hammer out our value proposition.

## VALUE PROPOSITION

A value proposition captures the essence of your product's unique benefit and how it solves a vexing customer problem, meets a critical need, or relieves severe pain better than anything else in the marketplace.

The most efficient path to profit is a value proposition that clearly delineates what your customer will get. Through experience, I've learned that a value proposition with a crystal-clear quantification of benefits is easiest to sell and the most compelling to buy. A Business-to-Business (B2B) value proposition is dominated by the quantification of hard benefits.

How you frame your value proposition can be different for B2B products than for Business-to-Consumer (B2C) products. While I believe that quantifying benefits is essential when selling to businesses, selling to consumers requires a heavier focus on qualitative benefits.

To define the benefits your value proposition will provide, ask questions that center on alleviating pain or providing a distinct advantage for your customer. A good way to craft your value proposition is to answer the following questions:

- Does your customer have substantial unserved needs—pain points?

- Does your product address your customer's unserved needs—does it resolve the pain?

- How much does the unserved need cost your customer—what is the cost of ongoing pain?

- How does your customer benefit from your product—what is the value of pain relief?

- Is your customer motivated to buy your product repeatedly—does it prevent recurring pain?

- Does your product serve a large and growing market—are there lots of customers in pain?

- Do you have a sustainable competitive advantage—do you have a unique solution to the pain?

# USI'S VALUE PROPOSITION

When I was thinking about forming USI, I knew our value proposition would be our dominant competitive advantage. Since our competitors sold their services on the strength of their brand name, using a traditional real estate services approach, the doorway was wide open for disruption. If we could show customers that they would receive quantified benefits many times greater than the cost paid, I was confident we would have a bankable value proposition.

USI's value proposition revolutionized the way corporations managed and controlled their corporate real estate. Corporations were suffering from high overhead costs, which dragged down their bottom lines. USI's solution resolved their pain by reducing real estate management and delivery expenses across the enterprise, saving them millions of dollars. We structured our outsourcing contracts as multiyear exclusives. By alleviating a major source of pain, USI enjoyed a 95 percent contract renewal rate, while maintaining a 20 percent net profit margin.

Developing a strong value proposition can ensure the growth and profitability of your new business. Invest the time to meet with prospective customers and advisors to test the merits of your value proposition up front. By patiently listening, you may be surprised at what you learn, and you might even walk away with a few preorders.

# THE IMPACT OF LISTENING

Too many entrepreneurs try to interact with customers through arm's-length relationships. This is almost always a mistake. Meeting with your customers face-to-face usually trumps any other kind of communication. You need to know your customers, their needs, their pain, and their expectations.

Whether you're starting a B2B or a B2C business, you need direct customer feedback to understand their reactions to your ideas. Ask thoughtful questions, and listen intently to the answers. You don't need professional focus groups or expensive surveys. You can gather this input yourself using a simple mock-up, a basic prototype, or a descriptive slide deck highlighting product features and benefits.

*Prepare yourself to learn by listening.* What do I mean by that? Don't listen with a preconceived notion of the outcome. Don't start formulating comments while the other person is talking. Clear your mind, and focus on everything your customer is saying. Take notes. Ask questions that will help you gain clarity. Let your prospective customer know you heard them.

Customers will tell you what they like and dislike about your product or service. You'll discover if you need to return to the drawing board or move forward with mass production. When you listen and confirm what you've learned, you are letting the customer know that you are thinking of their needs first. This process of listening, confirming, and adjusting heightens the customer's commitment to buy from you.

Treat your early customers as trusted advisors, and they will help you build your business. My early customers not only purchased USI's services; they provided critical advice on new service lines as USI grew.

## A BANKABLE BUSINESS MODEL

Once you've developed your idea and tested your value proposition, you need to determine how you will make money. Too often entrepreneurs fall in love with their idea but fail to have a business model worked out for how they will make a profit and generate sustainable cash flow. The business model is an amalgamation of all the component parts that make a business work: business vision, value proposition, operating plan, revenue model, production and distribution, and financial model. In short, a business model explains how your business will generate a profit.

Based on my experience with Baxter, I knew that USI would sell real estate outsourcing services to Fortune 1000 corporations. Corporations would outsource the management of their real estate portfolios to us, and we would become their single point of contact for all their real estate needs.

## OPERATING PLAN

USI's operating plan included three major components: sales, account management, and field execution.

### Sales

Initially, I would be the only salesperson. I had the responsibility to pursue leads, generate proposals, and close new business. Over the long haul, we planned to build our sales force on the ground and within driving distance of Fortune 1000 companies in the top 12 cities in the United States. (We discuss the importance of an aggressive sales function at length in chapter 8, "Sales Is a Contact Sport.")

Sales were vital to our growth, but we did not generate revenue until the contracts became operational. Once a contract became operational, our customers paid USI fixed fees to manage the account and transaction commissions to execute the work in the field.

### Account Management

Our business was organized to provide on-site account management at the customer's headquarters. The account teams would deliver centralized real estate management services. The initial service package would include transaction management and information management. As USI matured, we planned to expand our services to include strategic planning, project management, and facilities management. We would be paid a monthly advance (either fixed-fee, draw, or both) to cover the personnel costs directly associated with the account. If we received a draw, it would be repaid from transaction commissions.

### Field Execution

On the field execution side, we planned to share the commissions from landlords on all transactions with our customers. The commission-sharing arrangement would provide a unique cost-recovery benefit for the customer. This recovery benefit had the potential to cut the corporate real estate department budget in half.

## REVENUE MODEL

Your revenue model will determine how you price your goods and services. A key step in developing your revenue model is determining the types and sources of revenue your business will generate. Revenue types include product sales, service fees, advertising sales, data access fees, license fees, and/or commissions.

Each type of revenue generated can come from a multitude of sources. For example, sources of revenue can vary depending on customer type, including consumer, corporate, institutional, and/

or government; and procurement method, including direct sales, retail, online, and mobile. You should research pricing benchmarks for each type and source of revenue for your industry.

## USI'S REVENUE MODEL

We planned USI's revenue model to be based on contractual service fees and transaction commissions. USI would derive its revenues from midsize corporations. Given the complexity of the sale, USI would rely on a direct sales force to secure multiyear outsourcing contracts.

From my industry experience, I had a solid understanding of traditional pricing for real estate services. It was customary for each service to be priced and sold separately. The market was ripe for a new revenue model. USI's outsourcing solution consolidated all services into a package or bundle in exchange for volume-based pricing. I was confident USI's outsourcing approach could create significant value for the customer, underprice the competition, and generate a substantial profit.

Working out these details gave my partners and me confidence that we had a bankable business model. The next step was to quantify the model.

## REVENUE GENERATION

Once we figured out our revenue model, we needed to estimate revenue potential. We knew we would charge recurring service fees and event-driven transaction fees, but we needed to estimate annual transactions per account, so we developed a typical customer portfolio to quantify work requirements and transaction volumes. We tested the sample portfolio with "what if" calculations to determine revenue potential per account. Then we estimated the number of new account sales per year multiplied by the typical revenue potential per account.

Once you can explain your basic revenue and pricing model, you can estimate how many customers you expect to have, what they will purchase from you, and how often you will collect the revenue—daily, weekly, monthly, or annually. Taken together, this information will enable you to project your total revenue over time.

For a new business, recurring revenue streams provide more certainty of cash flow than event-driven revenue. After all, cash flowing into your business is your lifeblood. Given the extent of USI's resource commitment to each customer, we needed to negotiate multiyear exclusive contracts. We could not afford to worry about the peaks and valleys of one-off transactions. The multiyear contracts had the potential to create consistent revenue streams, making the business more easily scalable.

## PRODUCTION AND DISTRIBUTION

Once you have fleshed out your revenue model, you'll need to figure out what it will cost to create, manufacture, and deliver your product to your customers. For a manufactured product, you will need to think through and learn about your requirements for raw materials, labor, machinery, inventory, and distribution. For a service business, you'll need to look at how you will service your customers, including staffing, travel costs, response times, and performance reporting.

Since USI was going to be a service business, we were concerned about sales and service delivery costs. Beyond the production of proposals and due-diligence binders, we would not have a manufacturing cost. The key components of our product would be account management, data management, market knowledge, and negotiation skills. USI's expenses would be very similar to a traditional consulting business with our employees situated on-site at our customers' headquarters. In essence, we would replace a portion of the customer's real estate department at a lower cost, while improving customer service and generating a profit for USI.

A manufacturing and distribution business has a more significant challenge in accurately estimating production costs. It will be important to develop a thorough production cost model to ensure you have considered all of the major costs. Some of the factors you will need to address in order to estimate production costs include the following:

## Prototype costs

- How will you create a prototype or samples to help you secure preorders?

- How much will it cost to create a prototype or sample products?

## Production costs

- Quantify the type, amount, and source of materials, labor, and equipment needed to manufacture your product.

- Generate a preliminary estimate of costs for materials, labor, and/or equipment needed for your product.

- Determine whether you will make your product or outsource its production.

Determining accurate production costs and time frames for a manufacturing business is critical to the development of a profitable and reliable business model.

For new business owners who have never created a product or delivered a service, production and distribution can create unpleasant surprises. If you are unfamiliar with manufacturing processes and logistics, experienced advisors can be an invaluable resource, helping you to develop plans, determine requirements, and resolve uncertainties.

## MANAGING OVERHEAD AND GROWTH

We planned to grow the business carefully, keeping a tight grip on expenses. We agreed to a strict cost-control discipline. We would only increase overhead when we landed new business with new revenue streams. We referred to this expansion model as "simultaneous production and consumption," and stayed away from the riskier expansion model, "If we build it, they will come."

It seems that too many new business owners try to scale too fast. Instead of pacing their growth, they get ahead of themselves before truly understanding their business model and how they will make money. Many wind up launching, taking too much space, hiring too large a staff, and spending too much money on marketing before they have the revenue to support the costs. It is important to be prudent about managing and controlling overhead expenses.

## FINANCIAL MODEL

While developing our financial model, Gus, Tom, and I calculated various income statements and cash flow projections, using best, likely, and worst-case scenarios. Initially, we didn't even use spreadsheets; instead, we generated manual calculations to project profit and loss estimates. The numbers told us we would only need about five clients to be comfortably profitable. We planned for breakeven by the end of the first year, but it happened much faster than that, primarily because we underestimated the power of pre-selling.

In many respects, your financial model is an amalgamation of all of the revenues and costs associated with your business model. In order to build your financial model, you need to address all of the following questions:

- What can you charge for each unit or bundle of services?
- How many units you can reasonably expect to sell?
- What will it cost to make and deliver your product?
- How much will you spend on marketing and sales?
- How much will you be spending on support and overhead?
- How long will it take to reach breakeven?
- How much cash will you need to cover all your expenses?
- How long will it take to achieve sustainable profitability?

In the end, a business lives or dies by its cash flow and its profits. You need to test different pricing scenarios to achieve the right cash-flow outcome. Learn to be comfortable with numbers, even if you've never been before. The numbers tell the story of your business and give the clearest picture of its health.

## STRUCTURE

As we drew closer to launching USI, we met with Ridg Barker, our attorney, to help us form the appropriate legal structure. After considering the scale and potential size of USI, we studied the pros and cons of each alternative. Ridg guided me to form an S corporation rather than a C corporation. (The LLC form of enterprise had not yet been developed.) Unlike C corporations, S corporations pass corporate income, losses, deductions, and credits through to their shareholders for federal tax purposes, thus saving owners from double taxation.

Legally, a corporate structure limits personal liability, which is an essential protection in this litigious age. I strongly advise consulting with a qualified small business attorney before choosing the ideal structure for your business. Many lawyers will work out deals with startups to give you the legal help you need at a reasonable fee.

Incorporating would allow us to issue shares of stock to the founders. And later, as the company grew, it would provide us with the flexibility to issue stock to future partners and owners. The corporate form of organization can also smooth the way for various exit scenarios, such as going public or selling to another company. Although it is easier to form an LLC, depending upon the size of the business and the number of owners, the LLC form can be more complicated to manage in the long run. Your lawyer can help you select and contour the appropriate legal structure for your business.

To file the paperwork for incorporation, we needed to pick a launch date for our company. We also had to secure a taxpayer ID for the corporate entity and choose a state in which to incorporate. Since we were a small company operating out of Connecticut, we opted to file in Connecticut. Years later, we transferred from Connecticut and incorporated in Delaware for tax, governance, and flexibility advantages.

The company also needed its own checking account and bookkeeping system. Our accountant, Bill Turnof, advised that we start with a single-entry bookkeeping system, coordinated with our bank accounts. Eventually, we moved to QuickBooks to manage the complexities of our growing business.

Naturally, before you can incorporate and open a bank account, you need to select a name for your business. In chapter 4, "Entrepreneurial Branding," you'll learn how we chose our company name and set out to establish our brand.

## BE FLEXIBLE

Dynamic planning is just that—*dynamic*. As you deal with unknowns, learn new things, hit walls, overcome obstacles, and achieve goals, you need the flexibility to make adjustments and change your plans midstream. Unlike writing a formal business plan, a dynamic plan is a process that allows for the unrestricted ebb and flow of ideas in preparation for the launch of your new business.

## THE STARTUP ROADMAP

To ensure that you consider all of the variables for your dynamic plan, we have developed *The Startup Roadmap*. The *Roadmap* is divided into three categories: Proof, Profit, and Potential, as outlined below. *The Startup Roadmap* is included in appendix A. Use it to develop the dynamic plan for your business.

The contents of *The Startup Roadmap* are as follows:

### Proof

1. Business Idea
2. Distinctive Competence
3. Product Description
4. Market Opportunity

5. Target Customer

6. Value Proposition

7. Competitive Advantage

8. Preorders

## Profit

9. Business Model

10. Revenue Generation

11. Product Pricing

12. Production & Distribution

13. Creative Use of Technology

14. Marketing

15. Sales

16. Resource Requirements

17. Profit Validation

## Potential

18. Financial Projections

19. Cash Flow

20. Management Team

21. Future Growth

# 2

—

# LAUNCH AND EARLY STAGE

# 4

# ENTREPRENEURIAL BRANDING

Brand development was very personal for me. When launching USI, I wanted to create a brand that would leave a lasting imprint of my business in the minds of my customers. Our startup team worked to develop a brand that would stimulate interest and motivate prospective customers to seek out USI first. I believed that establishing a successful brand could work like gravity, pulling customers toward our company.

I call this process of brand development *entrepreneurial branding*. Entrepreneurial branding is complex and multidimensional. It will take time to think through all aspects of the branding process. You are creating a new entry in the marketplace. You will be judged on your brand's contribution—how well your brand meets your customers' needs. As an entrepreneur, your brand says everything about you: who you are, how you perform, and what you value. Entrepreneurial branding is built on trust and integrity, and it is measured by the strength and depth of enduring customer relationships.

Entrepreneurial branding is unique in two ways: First, the brand is a highly personal reflection of you and your business vision. Second, you must take full responsibility for the early stages of the branding process.

Entrepreneurial branding takes solid strategic thinking, grounded in basic marketing principles. The basis for a winning brand starts with your business idea and your value proposition—the problem that you are solving, how you will solve it, and the results your customers can expect.

Once the strategic foundation has been laid, then you can move on to developing the essential branding elements:

- Business name

- Tagline creation

- Logo development

- Customer awareness

- Customer service

Developing these branding elements played a significant role in establishing USI in the market and putting us on a path to early profitability.

## EVOLUTION OF THE USI BRAND

In the early 1990s, the US economy was in a recession, and corporate bottom lines were being squeezed. Corporations everywhere looked for ways to cut their overhead expenses and focus on their core business. They adopted a common rallying cry of "Do more with less." During this time of economic and financial turmoil, the concept of outsourcing noncore business activities took hold. When corporations decide to outsource, they rely on outside experts to create value by taking over noncore functions. Through outsourcing, businesses across the country saved millions by reducing staffing and related service costs. Since corporate real estate is a noncore function for most businesses, it was—and still is—ideally suited for outsourcing.

Based on my experience with Baxter, I felt confident that outsourcing the corporate real estate function would create significant value for the customer. Every corporation with more than 50 operating locations was a candidate for outsourcing. My company would be the first firm fully dedicated to outsourcing real estate services. We would integrate and manage all the essential parts of a corporate real estate department. Since the real estate services industry had been doing things the same way for decades, the concept of outsourcing had the potential to create a tidal wave of opportunity.

I felt certain that our value proposition would be a powerful magnet to the members of the C-Suite. Chief financial officers and heads of corporate real estate would be attracted to outsourcing because the savings would flow directly to the bottom line. My goal was to build a formidable brand based on this value proposition.

I started my branding process by considering some fundamental questions—ones that you should ask yourself as well:

- Are you building a B2B business or a B2C business?
- How would you classify your business?
    - Disruptive of the status quo?
    - Transformative through innovation?
    - Commodity-based with a differentiated approach?
    - Traditional with a proven business model?

- Can you describe your business idea clearly and succinctly?
  - What problem are you solving?
  - How will you solve the problem?
  - What results can the customer expect?
- Can you describe your value proposition?
  - Who is the customer?
  - What does the customer need?
  - How does your product create value?
- What is your business purpose and how is it different?

Armed with these answers, you can begin the brand-building process.

## NAMING YOUR BUSINESS

The name of your business should reflect your aspirations for your business. Your business name is the center point of your brand-building process. Answer the following questions to help figure out the name of your business:

- Does the name communicate your business purpose?
- Is the name clear, concise, and easily understood?
- Does the name communicate the potential scale of your business (local, national, global)?
- Does the name allow for the use of a meaningful acronym?
- Is the name memorable?
- Does the name describe your competitive advantage?

You should think long and hard about the image your business name will project. Just think about it: Every time you communicate with customers, you will use your name. Emails, your website, social media, business cards, letterhead, brochures, ads, and all forms of signage will carry your name. Make the name of your business count!

## NAMING USI

Naming United Systems Integrators Corporation (USI) was a complex and strategic decision. We knew that we would provide real estate outsourcing services to corporations through a central management system. We needed a business name that was hefty and global and communicated our competitive advantage.

We wanted the name to transcend people and time. Traditional real estate companies were named for their founders: Jones Lang LaSalle, Cushman & Wakefield, Coldwell Banker, and Trammell Crow. Utilizing my name might have served my ego, but it would not create the assurance that a large corporation would need to make a global award. We needed an institutional name, not an individual's name.

### The Logic Behind the Name

After spending years in the computer field with IBM and Hewlett-Packard, I wanted to apply lessons from the high-tech industry to the brick-and-mortar world of real estate. At the time, H. Ross Perot had disrupted the IT industry by creating the role of the "systems integrator." Perot convinced major corporations and government entities to outsource the management of all their IT systems to his company, EDS. EDS took the responsibility to integrate computer hardware, software, networks, and systems into a single unified solution for its customers.

It seemed clear to me that we could carve out the same role as a "systems integrator" in the business of corporate real estate services. Like EDS, we would take the responsibility to integrate and manage multiple services as a single-source provider. As such, we would provide the following:

- Strategy: aligning real estate with corporate strategy

- Transactions: site search & brokerage

- Architecture: space programming & planning

- Projects: construction & contract management

- Design: furniture, fixtures & equipment

- Facilities: operational support & maintenance services

- Information: operating real estate management systems

While I wanted to make systems integration the centerpiece of our name, I needed to communicate a global vision as well. At Trammell Crow, I serviced some very large, well-run multinational companies, including International Business Machines (IBM) and United Parcel Service (UPS). Both of these companies had built powerful, global brands around strong names with well-known acronyms. Also, in the case of UPS, I really liked the word *united*—bringing pieces together through a single source.

It all came together when I thought through the words, their meaning, and our business purpose. We would be an "integrator" of real estate services by "uniting" multiple disciplines through a single delivery "system." We named the business by putting these three words together: *United Systems Integrators*, thereby creating a solid acronym, *USI*, which would sell well with large corporations and could grow into a global brand.

Since we would be competing with the biggest real estate firms, we felt that United Systems Integrators Corporation connoted something formidable, lasting, and strong. At the same time, United Systems Integrators Corporation described something forward thinking, unique, and different—particularly in the brick-and-mortar world of commercial real estate.

As we worked toward the launch of our business, we became energized around our new name and acronym, United Systems Integrators Corporation (USI). We felt a sense of pride that would last long into the future. We had achieved our naming goal—and now we needed a meaningful tagline.

## DEVELOPING A TAGLINE

By combining your business name with a meaningful tagline, you have the opportunity to create the ultimate elevator pitch. Think about it. If you can develop a business name that introduces your unique advantage—combined with a tagline that clarifies your business purpose—then every time you send a message, you will be making a lasting impression. Said another way, the ideal combination of business name and tagline should communicate your *raison d'être*—your "reason for being."

When brainstorming your tagline, you should consider the following:

- Does it enhance your business name?
- Does it communicate your business purpose?
- Does it address the problem you are solving?
- Does it speak to your target customer?
- Is your tagline memorable and lasting?

Investing the time early on to think through your business name and a meaningful tagline can save hundreds of thousands of dollars in marketing and advertising expenses down the road. Here's how we labeled USI:

**United Systems Integrators Corporation**

*Serving Real Estate, Management,
and Information Needs*

To protect our name and tagline, we worked with our lawyer to conduct statewide and nationwide searches to ensure that our chosen name could be claimed and registered for our exclusive use. We considered an international search, but the cost and complexity were prohibitive for a startup. This due diligence started the process of protecting our intellectual property. Given all of the new media formats, it is imperative to search, claim, and register your name on all media platforms for your exclusive use.

## LOGO DEVELOPMENT

Once you have selected your business name and tagline, you will need to develop a logo that creates the appropriate visual image of your brand. A well-developed logo communicates a message about your company in a way that words alone cannot express. The logo includes the artwork or graphic image that integrates with your business name and tagline. Developing your logo includes selecting the style, fonts, colors, and sizes of the logo's elements. A well-designed logo will create an indelible impression in the mind's eye of your target customer. Your name, tagline, and logo are the beginning of your business reputation.

The logo for a B2B business is usually more formal and institutional, suited to attract the corporate decision maker within your target customer. The logo of a B2C business can be less formal and more personal, suited to appeal to the individual decision maker and buyer of your product.

A B2B logo includes developing an image that is—

- Substantive with a firm base in reality

- Important, meaningful, and significant

- Enduring, resilient, and attractive

A B2C logo includes developing an image that is—

- Stylish with a creative flair

- Friendly, easy, and enjoyable

- Appealing, memorable, and attention grabbing

## USI LOGO DEVELOPMENT

Since USI was focused on selling corporate real estate outsourcing to the C-Suite in large corporations, we needed a logo that communicated substance and staying power. Even though USI was a new company, we needed to convey the same steadfast image as a firm that had been around for a long time. Although I had a track record of success within the real estate services industry, I knew that large corporations would be reluctant to entrust substantial, multiyear outsourcing contracts to unproven startups. I believed that selecting the right logo would be critical to our success. I took my time.

One day, in Baltimore on business, I chose to stop in to visit my old friend and lifeguard buddy, Don Froude. Don worked for Alex. Brown & Sons. Alex. Brown was the first investment bank in the

United States, founded by Alexander Brown in 1800. It was a very successful company with a very strong brand name. When I walked in the lobby, I could feel the enduring strength of the firm's history.

When I sat down to wait for Don to come out of his office, I looked up and saw the Alex. Brown logo in a glass case. It was a war-torn red flag embroidered with a white B and a white horizontal stripe. The flag looked as if it had been through every battle since 1800. It had substance, heft, and was full of staying power. I loved it from the first moment I set eyes on it.

I knew that Alex. Brown did not own the rights to the flag logo, but they did own the right to the color, the stripe placement, and the single letter B on it. This would not be a concern for me because our flag would be so much different. I immediately started drafting images of a USI flag logo. Our flag would have a royal blue background with the letters "USI" emblazoned across the face with two white stripes beneath. We would also introduce a flagpole and design the flag to curl slightly as if blowing in the breeze.

I worked with a graphic designer to flesh out the details. It was a perfect image for our new B2B business. It fulfilled all of our logo development objectives. USI would "plant the flag" by winning large multiyear corporate outsourcing contracts with Fortune 1000 companies.

*USI flag logo*

I was always very proud of our name, our tagline, and our flag logo. Our logo always left a positive impression with our customers and stakeholders. I still love it today.

# BRAND IMAGE

Armed with your business name, your tagline, and your logo, you should consider investing in a graphic designer to integrate and package all of the pieces into a cohesive brand image. Just think about the number of design decisions that impact the development of your brand image: fonts, sizes, colors, shapes, depth, texture, highlights, placement, and graphic elements appropriate for different media formats.

At the same time, you will also need to select the best marketing platforms to build your brand, communicate your message, and attract new customers.

- Electronic Platforms
  - How do you want your name, tagline, and logo to look on your website?
  - What are the sizing implications on a mobile device?
  - How will your name, tagline, and logo integrate with your email?
  - Have you built in flexibility to address new media platforms?

- Social Media Platforms
  - How will you integrate your name, tagline, and logo with your blog?
  - How will you integrate your name, tagline, and logo in corporate email communications?
  - How will you integrate your name, tagline, and logo on LinkedIn, Facebook, Twitter, Instagram, Pinterest, and other social media platforms?

- o How will you integrate your name, tagline, and logo with streaming media?
- o How will you build in the flexibility to accommodate new social media platforms?

- Collateral Package
  - o How will you integrate your name, tagline, and logo into your business cards, letterhead, etc.?
  - o How will you represent your name, tagline, and logo in brochures and presentation materials?

- Event Marketing
- Advertising
- Signage

Your brand image is intellectual property. It needs to be protected with a trademark or a service mark and the associated legal registrations. You cannot afford to spend the time and money building your brand without having legal control.

## BUILDING CUSTOMER AWARENESS

Every day new options for raising customer awareness are being introduced. Your choices to engage with customers to build your brand seem almost limitless. Besides maintaining a website, writing a blog, and posting to social media platforms, mobile has opened the floodgates for interacting with customers. Tailor your platform selections to your product and target customer. Once you select your mix of platforms, you will need to dedicate resources to manage and maintain an active website, blog, social media, and mobile presence.

**Direct Email Marketing:** The most direct way to engage with customers is to secure their approval to receive direct email marketing from you. If you provide consistent, high-quality content to your target customers, they can be motivated to share their email addresses with you and maintain a welcome reception to your emails. Besides collecting qualified email addresses in exchange for valuable giveaways, many entrepreneurs are getting creative about marketing partnerships. If two noncompeting firms are pursuing the same target customer, establishing a joint email sourcing partnership can be an efficient way to open the door to new customers.

**Alternative Engagement:** In addition to joint partnerships, entrepreneurs are developing useful mobile applications and games to create dedicated connections with target customers. Streaming media for webcasts, podcasts, and webinars have become increasingly popular as the primary vehicle to keep the company's best salesperson—you—in front of the customer.

**Face-to-Face:** In addition to digital marketing efforts, you still need to budget, design, and produce an appropriate amount of face-to-face marketing programs including the following:

- Event-specific marketing programs
- Customer-networking forums
- Speaking engagements and meet-ups
- Customer-facing promotional campaigns
- Customer testimonials

Efficient use of your marketing dollars can be challenging, but purchasing keywords in pay-per-click advertising to drive qualified traffic to your business can be a valuable early spend.

The number of ways you can interact with target customers continually increases, but the brand-building challenge remains the same. You need to produce high-quality content that motivates your target customers to engage with you and your company.

## SUPERIOR CUSTOMER SERVICE

Your customers are your most precious asset. Your goal is to build a customer base of repeat buyers who promote your business to other buyers. An effective customer-referral system is the business equivalent of obtaining the Golden Fleece.

If you expect to build a powerful customer-referral system, you should have solid answers to the following questions:

- Do you deliver on your value proposition?
- Do you maintain a clear competitive advantage?
- Do you provide superior customer service?
- Do you make doing business together a pleasurable and rewarding experience?

Listed below are 10 key ingredients you can provide to deliver superior customer service:

1. Make a cultural commitment to superior customer service from the outset.

2. Assess, manage, and satisfy the customer at every single interface point.

3. Provide a significant product performance guarantee.

4. Assign a dedicated account manager to each customer relationship.

5. Be available 24/7 to log and address customer concerns.

6. Provide a 24-hour-response-time commitment.

7. Schedule customer engagement forums for feedback.

8. Reward team members for providing superior customer service.

9. Make sure that senior team members get directly involved with customers and lead by example.

10. Develop customer-feedback systems to stay in touch with customers and ahead of the competition.

## USI'S CUSTOMER SERVICE COMMITMENT

In addition to the 10 customer service points listed above, USI provided each account with dedicated on-site resources, ensuring personal service and immediate response time. We recognized that human error was inevitable. Rather than letting problems fester, we encouraged employees to acknowledge mistakes early. We would apologize quickly and, if appropriate, make reparation, rather than utilizing the courts to solve problems.

Our commitment to customer service enabled USI to enjoy a 95 percent contract renewal rate, while growing the business at a compounded annual rate of 40 percent. And we never entered a courtroom to resolve disagreements.

# BUILDING YOUR BRAND

As founder, you are the person most responsible for brand development. Your brand says everything about you: who you are, how you perform, and what you value. Entrepreneurial branding is a graphic reflection of your value proposition. It is built on trust and integrity, and is measured by the strength and depth of lasting customer relationships.

There are many facets to entrepreneurial branding. When you create a new entry in the marketplace, you will be judged on your brand's contribution. Take the time to think through all aspects of the branding process, including all the essentials we have covered in this chapter:

- Business name

- Tagline creation

- Logo development

- Customer awareness

- Customer service

While you are in the early stages of developing your brand, you should be assessing alternatives for startup funding. In the next chapter, we will discuss the startup funding process and how USI made its funding decision.

# 5

# CAPITAL, COST, AND CONTROL

Every business needs capital to start, operate, and grow. Every type of capital has a cost, with advantages and disadvantages to consider. And to some degree, every source of capital will affect the amount of control you will maintain over your business.

When I was starting USI, my accountant, Bill Turnof, counseled me to use *other people's money* (OPM), rather than risk my own.

"OPM, Eddie. OPM," Bill repeated every time we met.

Using OPM would limit my personal risk and enable me to expand my business beyond the limits of my personal resources. It would also give me the extra financial backing to take advantage of opportunities that could suddenly present themselves. However, I soon realized that using OPM could come at a very high cost in terms of business control and the relationships I would put at risk.

Should you use other people's money or your own money to transform your idea into a business? The funding alternatives within those categories are broad. Do you sell equity stakes to investors or borrow money? Or do you self-fund your business and bootstrap your way to profitability?

The decision you make will have a significant impact on the future of your business and the amount of control you will have over your business going forward.

*If you would like to plan for the capital you need to launch your business and evaluate funding alternatives, you can turn to* The Startup Funding Guide *in appendix B right now.*

## QUANTIFYING THE NEED

First, you need to determine your startup funding requirements.

When Gus, Tom, and I were planning the launch of USI, we produced numerous financial projections while holed up in the public library. We began by working out multiple revenue scenarios built on our outsourcing business model. First, we estimated how much money we could take in each month by managing the real estate portfolio for a medium-size corporation. We assumed a four-year outsourcing contract term and planned to charge a cost-plus fee for providing dedicated staffing at the customer's site. For the customer's real estate transactions, we planned to earn a commission for each transaction. Then we estimated how many transactions we could complete each month for the customer.

We cranked out the math to see how much revenue the medium-size portfolio could generate in a year. Once we had that model in place, we added the revenue streams from second, third, and fourth corporate customers. We developed conservative, aggressive, and moderate scenarios. We planned using the most conservative approach, even though we had a high degree of confidence that our preorders would turn into revenue-generating contracts.

We also planned to keep a stranglehold on expenses. During the first year, I wasn't going to draw any salary, and I was going to pay Gus and Tom with low salaries plus founders' equity. Thanks to Gus's site-search diligence, I was confident we could negotiate and prepay a short-term sublease on office space in a prime location. With a short-term sublease, we were able to keep our rent to less than 15 percent of our first-year operating budget.

If you are willing to scour the market, you can probably find a fully loaded sublease that includes office furniture. Just remember, the shorter the sublease term, the more aggressive you can be in negotiating the deal terms. Also, if another business is closing, you can usually purchase furniture and equipment from them at less than 25 percent of cost. Depending on your need, you can negotiate shared space or dedicated space using the same principles.

Beyond moderate salaries and rent, our projected costs included travel, marketing, phone, supplies, insurance, legal, and accounting. Naturally, we planned to keep even these costs to a minimum.

Once we secured the sublease and locked down salaries, we knew we would only spend money on revenue-generating activities that we were certain could make a profit. Following this rule is the surest way to put your business on a solid path to profitability.

When we factored in the timing of our projected cash inflow against our monthly spend, we figured that we needed about $100,000 to capitalize our venture with access to an additional $50,000 if our preorders did not quickly convert to revenue.

## OPM

When deciding if you should use other people's money, you need to consider the cost of the capital relative to your expected returns.

If you are planning to offer an ownership interest in your business in return for cash, you will need to create an expectation in the investors' minds that the business will be worth more in the future, and give them a better return on their investment, than if they invested their money elsewhere. If you decide to borrow the funds, you have to expect that your business will generate a return far greater than the cost of the loan. If this assumption is correct, using leverage (i.e., debt financing) to grow your business could pay off handsomely.

Finding outside investors or lenders for a business that is still in the idea stage and has no revenue can be very tough. Despite what you may read in the media about angel investors and venture capitalists (VCs) funding startups, the most common route for entrepreneurs seeking OPM is to approach the people they know best—friends and family. However, one problem in approaching friends and family is that friends and family know you best. After all, friends and family certainly value your strengths but also have direct experience with your weaknesses.

Entering a round of fund-raising with friends and family can make sense if the people who invest or lend you money have experience with startups. It can also make sense if they have useful knowledge they can contribute to the business, such as high-value connections, technical skills, and/or relevant industry knowledge.

## Friends and Family—Equity

Because I trusted my accountant's advice, I first decided to try raising startup capital using OPM, together with my own savings. I put together a shortlist of wealthy friends and family members whom I thought would be interested in writing me checks in return for an interest in USI. Yet, I knew that each share of equity I sold would introduce investment risk to my friends and family. It would also open me up to questions about my business decisions and trade away a portion of my future control, growth, and profits.

Before you decide to raise equity funding, you need to ask yourself how much control you are willing to give up. In addition, because equity investors will have no direct claim on any assets in the event of a failure, you should be sure that your potential investors understand that they risk losing all of their investment if your company does not succeed.

The more I thought about asking those closest to me to risk their hard-earned savings on my startup idea, the more uncomfortable I became. If USI failed, my friends and family could lose an important part of their savings. How could I live with that? If their investment was less than five percent of their assets, and they were experienced investors, I would feel okay. But if they had never made an investment in a startup before and were risking 10 percent or more of their liquid savings, I just knew I couldn't take the money.

More importantly, I began to wonder if anyone on my list could bring meaningful value to the business besides money. I knew that none of the investors on my shortlist shared the knowledge and experience I had in real estate outsourcing. Furthermore, they did not have the complementary skills needed to move the business ahead. And finally, none were entrepreneurs. How could they possibly appreciate the fire that was burning within me? How could they fairly assess the risks and the opportunities of my new venture?

I also wondered if any of the investors would take their ownership interest a little too seriously. By giving up a percentage of the business to my investors, I could be ceding my right to call the shots. Some equity investors are passive, trusting you to make the right decisions. But others will look over your shoulder, expect regular updates, and want to have a say in how you run your business.

I was leaving the corporate world so that I could control my own destiny and succeed or fail on my own terms. If investors started second-guessing me, I knew there could be conflict ahead. That conflict can, and often does, result in those highly valued relationships falling apart.

There were just too many *ifs*. I finally decided that I did not want to risk the chance of causing permanent damage to my personal relationships. For me, the option to raise equity financing from friends and family was out.

### Friends and Family—Debt

What about asking them for a loan? Friends and family fund-raising rounds are often completed as unsecured loans to the entrepreneurs. Depending on the terms of the agreement, lenders may have a claim on business assets and on the revenue the business produces, but they are not owners. I wouldn't have to give up any control, and none of my personal assets would be placed at risk; I would simply have the obligation of paying off the loan. But even then, I knew I would feel deeply responsible for any savings my friends or family members could lose if I were not able to repay the loan. If you do ask family or friends for a loan to start or grow your business, make sure they understand that they may lose the entire value of their loan.

Self-funding was beginning to look better and better to me. But first, I had one more avenue I wanted to explore—securing a small business loan.

### Small Business Loans

I had a solid relationship with our local bank and a fair amount of my personal savings in an account there. The bank took pride in being a hometown bank, providing services and financing for area residents and businesses. I also had excellent credit and a record of making good on all my obligations, so I fully expected to be met with open arms.

To my amazement, the loan officer greeted me with a stop sign. She told me the bank normally did not make loans to startups. However, because of my long-standing relationship, the bank president said they would consider a loan and proceeded to give me a boatload of paperwork to fill out. Before they would talk further, I had to produce pro forma income statements and balance sheets for my proposed business, personal tax returns, and my bank statements. I also had to submit a business plan.

Suddenly, I was faced with a lot of additional planning work that took me off course. I wanted to put my time and energy into starting my business, not filling out forms or writing detailed plans on the slim chance of getting the loan. But any provider of capital, whether they are a professional equity investor or loan provider, will insist on receiving similar business documentation. The business plan doesn't have to be lengthy, but it must answer all the bankers' basic business questions and demonstrate sound financial planning.

Once I produced the paperwork, I was surprised that the bank would only make a loan that was *fully collateralized* by my savings account. In addition, the interest rate I would have to pay on the loan was substantially more than the interest the bank was paying me on my savings. That seemed crazy to me, so I looked to other sources.

## SBA Loans

Next, I tried a Small Business Administration (SBA) lender. The SBA promoted itself as a friend of small business, offering startups easy access to capital. The SBA doesn't make the loan, but they back the bank, which makes the loan if the borrower passes the SBA screening process.

Unfortunately, the SBA lenders were no more welcoming than my bank and made me jump through similar hoops. However, the SBA did not require fully collateralized loans. Instead, in many cases, they were willing to take some risk and bet on the promise of the business. Even so, the SBA wanted to understand the business model, the financial projections, and the economic conditions affecting the business.

I was highly conservative by nature and didn't want to overpromise on USI's ramp-up to profitability. Since my integrity was at stake, and I prided myself in meeting all my commitments, I presented the worst-case scenario. The financial model I submitted projected USI burning through $300,000 before reaching breakeven in its third year. The SBA lender did not like that. They wanted to see USI achieving breakeven in 18 months or less.

Furthermore, because of the commercial real estate meltdown in the early 1990s, the SBA lenders considered any business remotely related to real estate to be toxic. They couldn't see the difference between our outsourcing business model and the failing business models in the real estate development sector. When the SBA lenders said they wanted to study my application for three to six months before giving me an approval, I realized that an SBA loan was out of the question too. I was chomping at the bit to get going.

If you try to get a small business loan, the decision time will probably be shorter than I experienced, but you will be faced with similar roadblocks. Be prepared to do a lot of homework and to give the lending institution your personal guarantee that the loan will be paid back. If your business is a startup, and you choose a traditional commercial lending source, you will have to put up personal assets to collateralize the loan.

# YOUR OWN MONEY—BOOTSTRAPPING

After my experience with the banks, I knew that using my own money was the best funding route for me. Rather than getting tied up in red tape, I began to feel more comfortable putting my own assets at risk. I could maintain ownership control and would only have to answer to myself. Using only savings as startup capital and foregoing a salary for the first year, I would bootstrap USI's growth by reinvesting all of the profits into the business.

Because Barbara and I had been saving up to purchase a house, we had built up a substantial nest egg. After months of debating the startup and funding decisions, we finally agreed to make the sacrifice and shift our priorities from buying a house to investing our savings in the business. If you have the financial wherewithal, I feel strongly that using your own money to fund your new business is the best path to take.

Deciding to bootstrap is a big step. There are real trade-offs and opportunity costs to consider:

- Do you have the personal resources to invest in your business without betting the ranch?

- Are you comfortable putting your own money at risk to fund a brand new enterprise with an unknown outcome?

- Can you accept the fact that the money you invest in your business will no longer be available for personal contingencies such as buying a car, buying a home, funding education, dealing with unplanned medical expenses, or saving for retirement?

- What if the business fails? Can you withstand such an outcome?

## PERSONAL SACRIFICE

To minimize the risks of bootstrapping, Barbara and I came to the conclusion that we needed to downsize the cost of our personal life.

With no salary coming in, and our savings flowing out, we had to figure out how much money our family needed to survive. To build in a significant margin for safety, we planned to cut our family's expenses in half. After careful calculations, we realized that if we moved from our four-bedroom house to a two-bedroom cottage, we could cut our rent and occupancy expense by 60 percent. Barbara and I also agreed to eliminate all luxuries and minimize the cost of essentials. After making these reductions, we were confident we could survive for almost three years just living off our savings.

Barbara gave the plan her full support and agreed to manage USI's finances without compensation. She knew me well and had faith in my ability to start the business and succeed. Even though the perks of a partner's income and benefits at Trammell Crow were a lot to give up, Barbara understood that I would never be truly happy until I left the corporate fold and started my own business.

Her support was particularly meaningful because she was familiar with the road ahead. Barbara had grown up in a farming community along the Mississippi Delta. Her parents ran a truck stop in Arkansas, where she had learned all about long days, hard work, and sacrifice—all vital ingredients of a successful business.

Whether you are single, in a relationship, or married, you need to determine together how much of your savings you will consume to survive during the startup phase. What is the bare minimum you need to live on during the first three years? What can you do without? Then, make sure your spouse, partner, or significant other is willing to take the risk with you, make the sacrifice, and support whatever it takes to succeed.

When you use your own money, fear of failure becomes your greatest motivator. I was desperate for success, and I was going to do everything I could to ensure that my business would prosper.

## BOOTSTRAPPING IS BEST

When I was starting USI, I couldn't wait to lift off. I had quit my job and felt impatient to get started. I considered sourcing money from friends and family but could not rationalize the risk of damaging personal relationships or losing control of my business. So I pursued debt financing from commercial banks and the SBA, only to get ensnared in the red tape of institutional decision-making. In the end analysis, I realized that bootstrapping was the only pathway that would enable me to maintain full control of my business.

*To help you learn more about evaluating, planning, and sourcing capital for your business venture, we have included* The Startup Funding Guide *in appendix B.*

*The Startup Funding Guide* covers all of the following topics:

1. Determining Your Funding Requirements

2. Building Your Financial Model
   - Planning Cash Expenditures for Assets
   - Understanding the Impact of Cash Flow
   - Developing Your Financial Projections

3. Acknowledging the Cost of Capital: Equity & Debt

4. Developing and Delivering Your Pitch

5. Understanding the Investor's Point of View

6. Determining Your Source of Funding
   o Other People's Money—Equity or Debt
   o Your Own Money—Bootstrapping
   o Beyond Friends, Family, & Banks

7. Making the Right Funding Decision

Once you have made a funding decision, it's time to mobilize your plans, launch your new business, and begin to convert your preorders into revenues. The next chapter is dedicated to the discipline of implementation and execution.

# 6

# "DO IT! DO IT! DO IT!"

It's one thing to plan a new business, but starting the business is the step that really counts. Launching and growing your business takes incredible dedication and stamina. It requires going the extra mile to make new sales, attract new customers, and build on the customer relationships you already have by fulfilling every commitment on time, on budget, and at the quality level your customers expect. Your business is your baby—it demands devoted care and regular feeding. Much like raising a child, you will do whatever it takes to help your baby succeed. Your most significant challenge will be to balance customer development activities with business growth initiatives, including

- Cultivating experienced advisor relationships
- Monetizing your business model
- Turning preorders into contracts

- Deepening customer relationships
- Investing in growth catalysts
- Hiring superior talent
- Relentlessly pursuing growth

## CULTIVATING EXPERIENCED ADVISOR RELATIONSHIPS

Once I had settled on USI's business model, made the decision to bootstrap, and completed our corporate filing, we were ready to finalize the process of signing our sublease. Tom, Gus, and I drove to our new office to meet with our sub-landlord, John Stanger. John was subletting the space to us because he and his business partner were shutting down their private equity firm, Stanger Miller. They had been very successful, but they wanted to go out on top and enjoy the results of their efforts.

John and I hit it off right way. As we were signing the lease and handing over the check, we started talking about John's career. Much to my surprise, I learned that he had been the head of General Electric Credit, the precursor to the megafinance unit, GE Capital Corporation.

Knowing that John had come from such a high perch in the corporate world, I was keenly interested in learning why he had become an entrepreneur and started his own firm. John grimaced and said, "Every waking minute was planned, scheduled, and booked for me while I was an executive at GE." Then he smiled and said, "By starting my own business, I made more money, and I had more freedom than I ever had working for someone else."

Hearing this energized me even more about starting my own company. If a past chief operating executive from General Electric was fired up about starting up, then someone like me had nothing to lose.

During our conversation, I asked him for three points of advice about launching our new company. I will never forget John's simple, straightforward, and unwavering advice: "Do it! Do it! Do it! You can build more wealth and have more fun running your own business than in a lifetime spent in the corporate world." He closed by saying, "I know it, because I did it."

I was never more excited about building USI into a successful business. At the time, I thought my meeting with a senior executive like John Stanger was an anomaly. However, I would soon discover that the person in the office next door was a gentleman by the name of Dick Munro, past chairman and CEO of Time Warner. To my surprise, Dick was open to meet with me and impart his wisdom and share his connections. (I discuss my experience and Dick Munro's advice points in chapter 7, "A Hard Lesson.")

It seemed almost every day I was developing influential new relationships, which helped propel us toward our business goals. Once you venture out on your own, all kinds of new doors will open up. Challenge yourself to go through those doors to create connections that can literally change the trajectory of your success.

## MONETIZING YOUR BUSINESS MODEL

As soon as we moved into our office, I turned my focus to generating revenue. At that point, my savings were flowing out to pay our rent, pay my staff's salaries, and pay for our other overhead expenses. Verbal promises from prospects to do business together were one thing, but we needed to turn those preorders into signed contracts. We had to get the cash flowing to help cover our costs.

I stayed up late worrying that Patterson Dental and IDS had talked about doing business—but would they convert into paying customers? Would they each provide USI with a bona fide, signed contract?

Although John Stanger had left behind his phone system, the telephone company had not yet turned on our service and given us a number. Since we did not have cell phones, I went downstairs with a pile of change to call Minneapolis long distance on the pay phone in our building's lobby. Standing at the public phone, I got Bill Scheller at Patterson Dental on the line. After a few pleasantries, I asked, "Bill, can we get a contract?"

Bill was encouraging. He told me he was coming to Stamford the following week, and we could meet to put the contract together.

## PATTERSON'S GROWTH CHALLENGE

I knew that Patterson's challenge was to consolidate 35 small distribution centers into seven large ones located near major UPS delivery hubs. Bill had been the architect of the consolidation plan. The proximity to UPS hubs would enable Patterson to guarantee overnight delivery to dentists all over the country.

Patterson's new distribution centers would be in Pennsylvania, Florida, Texas, Indiana, Washington, California, and Minnesota. The project would require multiple steps including renting distribution space, procuring land and building new space, disposing of old space, and consolidating inventory from the small sites into Patterson's new distribution centers.

Patterson's redesign of its distribution centers catered to the needs of dentists as small business owners. The dentists could not afford to carry the cost of the inventory, nor pay for the space to store it. Yet they needed a reliable supply line with next-day delivery to secure expensive items such as drills, drill bits, and molds. When Barbara heard about Patterson's plans, she explained to me the genuine need Patterson would be filling for dentists with next-day delivery.

## TURNING PREORDERS INTO CONTRACTS

When I met with Bill, he was incredibly enthusiastic about working with USI on Patterson's consolidation plan. Together, we crafted a project-based contract for the initial site search. We signed the agreement on USI's 45th day in business on October 15, 1991.

We immediately went to work on the Pennsylvania distribution center for the Northeast corridor. Once we completed our due diligence, built our financial models, and short-listed the alternatives, we scheduled our next meeting at Patterson's headquarters in the Twin Cities.

There, I would be making the presentation with Bill Scheller to Pete Frechette, Patterson's CEO, and Ron Ezerski, the CFO. In addition to presenting our recommendation for the Pennsylvania distribution center, I would be attempting to grow the account by asking for the exclusive contract for all Patterson's distribution centers.

Upon arriving in Minneapolis, I realized immediately that Patterson Dental had a warm and friendly culture. Even though the building's exterior looked like a warehouse, the atmosphere inside was homey, as if it housed a big family. The company offered free lunch, and everyone sat in the same lunchroom, even the members of the C-Suite.

My presentation went very well. It turned out that Bill had an excellent rapport with both Pete and Ron. It became clear very quickly that Bill had invested the time to build senior-level sponsorship to expand the contract with USI. It also helped that Pete had been an executive at Baxter Healthcare, enabling him to verify my credentials with his friends at Baxter. Still, Patterson's executives were not about to award an exclusive contract to a startup.

PATTERSON

Patterson Dental Company
1100 East 80th Street
Minneapolis, Minnesota 55420
(612) 854-2881
FAX: (612) 854-8381

October 15, 1991

Ed McLaughlin
President
United Systems Integrators Corporation
300 First Stamford Place
Stamford, Connecticut    06902

Dear Ed:

     I would like to thank you for helping me put together the partnership between the Patterson Dental Company and United Systems Integrators Corporation.  This working relationship will combine the strengths of both of our companies as we continue our site search projects.  As your first client, we want you and the employee's of USI to know that we support you through this start up phase.  For your information, The Patterson Dental Company is employee owned.  As an ESOP company, we truly believe in a phrase that we use, "Pride in Ownership".  Based on our association over the past year and your exceptional work to date, we have confidence that your client list will grow.

     In accordance with our agreement, Patterson Dental requests that USI commence site acquisition consulting work on both the Eastern Region Project and Midwest Region Project.  In addition, we request that USI begin the disposition consulting project on the Eastern Regional facilities outlined in our agreement.

     To strengthen this partnership and to insure that Patterson receives the maximum benefit from our exclusive agency relationship with USI, we believe that it is extremely important that USI provide Patterson's sole representation in the local market.  If any questions arise concerning the working relationship between Patterson Dental Company and USI or our commitment to USI as our sole representative and exclusive agent, please refer these questions to me for clarification at 612-854-2881.

Sincerely,

Patterson Dental Company

William K. Scheller
Director of Distribution

*An Employee Owned Company*

*Patterson contract award letter*

Instead, they gave USI approval to complete the Pennsylvania project and to begin work on the Midwest and Southern distribution centers. Once we had proven our competence, we felt confident that Patterson would award USI the exclusive contract for all of its distribution centers, as well as for all of its sales offices. This would be a huge victory for USI.

Looking back, I believe Pete Frechette and Ron Ezerski felt a similar entrepreneurial spirit in me. After all, Pete had stepped away from Baxter, and Ron had stepped away from a successful accounting career, to expand Patterson Dental into a single-source provider of dental products to dentists all across America. Additionally, Bill knew the USI story would be a solid fit with Patterson's leadership. After all, upstarts support upstarts because they can appreciate their values, motivations, and goals. We both respected each other's desire for control and willingness to take the responsibility to make decisions and live with the outcomes.

## DEVELOPING CUSTOMER RELATIONSHIPS

It is important to recognize that trust is earned and re-earned every single day. To build trust with your customers, I recommend that you take the following actions:

- Develop an advocate or coach within the customer organization.

- Ensure your product's benefits align with your customers' needs.

- Work together to formulate plans to solve problems.

- Jointly develop and sign contracts for trial work.

- Exceed customers' expectations on every assignment.

- Jointly market your success within the C-Suite.

- Execute a master contract for an exclusive relationship.

Prior to securing the exclusive contract for all of Patterson's real estate services, we had to prove we could do the work on time, on budget, and at a quality level that exceeded Patterson's expectations. Gus went to the local market in central Pennsylvania to complete the first phase of due diligence. Since UPS could provide overnight shipping to the Northeast corridor from Harrisburg, Lancaster, or York, Gus analyzed every available option in each of those markets.

Once Gus had documented his findings, we coordinated with Bill to meet in the market to tour the properties and make a shortlist of the best options. Based on Patterson's needs, we targeted Lancaster as the ideal distribution point. Bill was a hands-on manager and joined us in the lease negotiations.

Up to this point, USI's service delivery expenses had been limited to mileage costs and a few meals. To Bill's credit, he recognized our startup budget limitations and offered to share his hotel room to minimize our overnight expenses. We were "lean and mean" in a Hampton Inn with two beds and a pullout couch.

When we completed the project, we had struck a deal on Patterson's behalf to lock in the property for 20 years. When the head of sales for Patterson came to Lancaster and saw what we had accomplished, he said to Bill, "Those guys really know what they are doing." That was the beginning of a beautiful relationship.

Our next project for Patterson was in Northern Indiana. It just so happened that Northern Indiana was the only location that could serve to deliver overnight packages to Chicago and Detroit. Gus had to research every available distribution location in the northern half of Indiana—a tall order by any standard.

After three weeks in the market, it became clear that South Bend would be the ideal location. Since there was plenty of available land, but few good choices of existing warehouse and distribution space, we asked Patterson if we could develop the building for them from the ground up. At first, Patterson's management was hesitant, but after reviewing our findings, they agreed that USI should build the company's new distribution center. This decision was a major advance in our relationship with Patterson and introduced a profitable new service line for USI—buying land and developing buildings.

As an aside, while we were in South Bend developing Patterson's building, we visited the Notre Dame campus and tried to sneak onto the football field. We were held up at the gates because they were filming a movie, *Rudy*, which has become one of the top sports movies of all time. This underdog story rings true with many entrepreneurs.

## THE ALLIANCE NEGOTIATION

Similar to our experience in Indiana, we could not find any existing distribution space in north Texas proximate to the UPS distribution hub that was suitable for Patterson's needs. After an extensive site search throughout the Dallas/Fort Worth Metroplex, we decided to pursue a land purchase at the newly formed Alliance Airfield Development just north of Fort Worth. The land had been assembled by Ross Perot Jr. to operate as a logistics hub anchored by an airfield. The hub was dedicated to freight transport by air, rail, and truck to distribute products throughout the southern corridor of North America.

If we were successful, Patterson Dental would be one of the first companies to locate their distribution center at Alliance. Remember, this was in the early 1990s, when the country was submerged in surplus commercial real estate, and Alliance needed tenants to validate their concept. The Alliance team was very interested in developing a build-to-suit and leasing it to Patterson. Bill Scheller and I felt very comfortable that Patterson's distribution needs would be well served at Alliance—but we wanted to buy the land and build for Patterson's ownership. Both Alliance and Patterson wanted to control the land, which was setting things up for a very tough negotiation.

Bill and I met at Ross Perot Jr.'s office in North Dallas to begin the negotiation. Since the Alliance Development was in its early stages, Ross Jr. was directly involved. It was a very exciting time to be meeting with him for numerous reasons: First, Ross Jr. had recently become the first man to pilot a helicopter around the world; second, I had modeled USI after EDS, which had been founded by his father, Ross Perot Sr.; and third, Ross Sr. had been running as an independent candidate for president of the United States.

Ross Jr. and I hit it off quite well. I shared the USI story and its connection to the EDS model as a systems integrator. He was very inquisitive and complimentary, asking, "Did you bootstrap this business on your own? That is very impressive." I knew his comments came from direct experience since the Perots met regularly with entrepreneurs seeking funding for new ventures. I felt a renewed sense of pride and an even greater commitment to succeed, no matter the sacrifice.

We picked up the dialogue about Patterson's needs and then flew in Perot's private helicopter to the Alliance Airport in Fort Worth to tour the sites and begin the negotiations. The negotiations were tense from the get-go since we both wanted to "own the dirt." The discussions came to an impasse, and we parted without an agreement, since neither party would budge.

We stayed in contact and argued long distance about the business terms. We knew we needed one another to succeed. Alliance wanted new business occupants for validation, and Patterson wanted to own its operating location at Alliance to achieve its business objectives. Ultimately, Alliance agreed to allow Patterson to purchase the land with the understanding that Alliance would build the distribution center to Patterson's specifications. Now we needed to agree on the

purchase price for the land and building, setting off another round
of hard negotiations.

H. R. PEROT, JR.
1700 LAKESIDE SQUARE
12377 MERIT DRIVE
DALLAS, TEXAS 75251

December 17, 1992

Mr. Ed McLaughlin
President & CEO
United Systems Integrators Corporation
1055 Washington Blvd., Fourth Floor
Stamford, Connecticut 06901

Dear Ed:

Thank you for taking the time to visit with me.

The Alliance program has moved very quickly over the
last four years. One of the reasons for its success
is the strength of the partnerships we have formed
with public and private entities.

I am excited about our partnership with Patterson
Dental. We will move quickly and efficiently to
satisfy your facility needs.

I hope you and your family have a Happy Holiday
Season! I look forward to our next visit.

Sincerely,

H.R. Perot, Jr.

HRPjr/ss

*Follow-up letter from Ross Perot Jr.*

To break the logjam, we both agreed to a final "pass or play" decision process. We wrote down our best purchase price on a napkin
and passed it across the table to the Alliance Team. They had to
flip the napkin over and decide to "pass or play" without further

negotiation. When they saw the number, Alliance agreed to do business. This was the beginning of a long-term relationship.

## EARNING THE EXCLUSIVE

Based on our success with Patterson in Pennsylvania, Indiana, and Texas, Patterson contracted with USI to be the sole provider of all of their distribution centers and sales offices. This contract gave USI the exclusive right to represent Patterson on every transaction and construction project for their entire real estate portfolio. This was a huge coup for our two-year-old startup.

USI earned the exclusive through patient execution and by building a record of success on every single project. You can achieve similar results by applying the following principles:

- Recognize that your reputation will be defined by your customers' satisfaction.

- Focus and overinvest to achieve superior results.

- Communicate at regular intervals to ensure alignment.

- Realize that trust is earned and re-earned every day.

- Build and maintain direct contact with the C-Suite.

- Set realistic expectations and consistently overperform.

- Ask for the exclusive when you have earned your right to it.

## INVESTING IN GROWTH CATALYSTS

We were well on our way to executing our plan and meeting our goals. We had launched USI in September of 1991, and we were cash-flow positive four months later. We had succeeded in turning our first preorder into an exclusive contract with Patterson Dental. In addition, our second preorder had turned into a multimarket contract with IDS American Express. Locking in multiple recurring revenue streams was instrumental to our rapid ramp-up to profitability. After three years, we expanded from three founding partners to 18 full-time employees, and we needed more resources to keep up. Then I received a fortuitous phone call from a past Trammell Crow field partner named Rick Bertasi.

## A Little History

During my days with Trammell Crow, I had the opportunity to work with Rick in pursuit of a major real estate services contract with Hewlett-Packard in Northern California. Rick was a member of the Trammell Crow development office in Sacramento. He was extraordinary. Rick had a Dartmouth MBA combined with Wall Street experience. He was smart, articulate, and tireless. I knew about his tenacity because we had worked together in the trenches, pulling all-nighters and creating complex proposals.

After my experience with Rick in the field, I suggested to my Trammell Crow management that we recruit him to join our National Marketing team. I felt strongly that he would be an excellent fit in our small group, but management did not go along with my recommendation.

# HIRING SUPERIOR TALENT

I felt as though "lightning struck twice" when Rick called. Sure enough, the door opened once again for me to work with Rick. But this time, I was in the decision-making seat, and I wasn't going to miss this opportunity. I picked up Rick's call in hopes that he was available. Rick started out by saying, "I understand you're building a services company. I'm planning on relocating to the East Coast, and I'm looking at new opportunities."

This was music to my ears. I immediately put on the full-court press to recruit Rick. I just knew he could help catapult USI's growth. Our first meeting lasted for almost 10 hours straight. We didn't even stop for lunch. We discussed the business plan, the business strategy, growth plans, and Rick's potential role and responsibilities, including compensation and equity participation. We were both excited about the potential of working and creating value together. I knew Rick would bring his own distinctive competencies to the company.

## Strategic Leadership

When Rick joined USI in January of 1994, he quickly put a turbo charger on new business development. He landed new relationships with Pitney Bowes in Stamford, Centex in Dallas, First Union in Charlotte, GMAC in Philadelphia, and Manpower in Milwaukee, to name a few. In addition to landing strategic accounts in different markets around the United States, Rick fine-tuned our business model, recruited and trained new staff, upgraded our sales materials, and played a key role in the development of our proprietary customer-facing software, Sequentra. Ultimately, Rick was promoted to president of USI Companies and became the second-largest equity owner in the company.

Rick was a very strong leader and contributor. He was not afraid to challenge anyone, including customers, employees, and me. Rick made our company better, but on numerous occasions, I had to swallow my ego and smooth the sentiments of other colleagues who were not as comfortable with Rick's style. An important lesson for my fellow entrepreneurs is to hire truly great people, even at the expense of your pride. As long as I kept my own ego in check, the decision was easy—Rick made our company more valuable.

## Product Line Expansion

Listening to our customers and adapting our business model to meet their needs were top priorities. Just before Rick joined USI, we had the good fortune to land an exclusive real estate service contract with the Olsten Corporation on Long Island. Olsten was a high-growth temporary service firm competing with the likes of Manpower and Kelly Services. Olsten had hundreds of offices throughout the United States. USI was tasked with the responsibility to find, negotiate, and open new Olsten office locations. We also built and managed Olsten's real estate information database.

We reported to Bill Constantini, General Counsel of the Olsten Corporation. Bill was an innovator. Once Bill understood the mechanics of USI's business model and the control points in the contract, he gave USI the freedom to get the job done. He extended trust, and we overperformed to earn and maintain it. We met with Bill on a monthly basis to review progress, address issues, and discuss Olsten's business needs.

At one of our meetings, Bill highlighted Olsten's need for services beyond finding offices. He stressed that local Olsten field managers needed help planning office layouts, building out the space, and furnishing it. Bill wanted USI to solve the problem by providing turnkey services for design, space planning, and project management. If we could organize the resources, this new service line could become a substantial new product line. I agreed to do the work, but we needed to find an architect to mastermind the design and implementation.

Simultaneously with the Olsten meetings, I had been pitching for a piece of IBM's business. Along the way, I met with one of IBM's in-house architects named Tina Casolo. As we talked about USI and our plans for expansion, Tina suggested that I meet with her husband, Michael. Michael owned an architecture and design firm in the town where I lived. He had a degree in architecture from Notre Dame and had studied urban planning and real estate at Columbia. Michael was very competent and competitive with a deep understanding of design and construction.

## Line of Business Management

When I met Michael, we had an instant rapport. Michael quickly grasped my vision and USI's tremendous growth potential. After numerous discussions, combined with an aggressive offer that included equity, Michael decided to shut down his own business to join USI in late 1994. That's how much he believed in our model, our potential, and his own ability to add value to our business. Once on board, Michael developed a plan to fulfill Olsten's design and construction needs and then recommended that we offer a similar suite of services to all USI customers.

Michael was free to develop his own operating plan, leveraging USI's business model and relationship base to sell design and construction services. He developed a flexible pricing model including cost per square foot, cost per hour, and cost per project, with dedicated resources priced on a cost-plus basis. Under Michael's leadership, USI's service lines expanded to include space programming, space planning, project management, furniture management, signage, and workplace consulting. Each service line was managed as a profit center, which rolled up into USI's Design and Construction P&L.

USI became the first real estate outsourcing firm to offer comprehensive design and construction services. Michael's contribution played a significant role in USI's profitability and penchant for expansion. Michael was an entrepreneur in his own right. He needed the freedom to take control, organize, and build his own business within USI.

As you grow your business, invest the time to listen to your customers. Your customers will tell you about their problems and help you to figure out the best way to solve them. Then hire entrepreneurial people who will listen, observe, innovate, and execute. Once you have them on board, listen to their ideas, and let them lead and build in their areas of distinctive competence. Give your leadership the opportunity to challenge the status quo and create genuine change. They will take you to places you never thought possible.

## GEOGRAPHIC EXPANSION

By 1996, we had landed key accounts with dedicated on-site teams in many major cities east of the Mississippi River. At the same time, we were executing more real estate transactions and construction projects in Los Angeles, San Francisco, and Seattle. It was time to build a dedicated management team on the West Coast.

My old friend Henry Johnson, who had originally recruited me into Trammell Crow, contacted me about his Harvard Business School classmate from Los Angeles. His friend's name was Nick Westley. Nick had recently concluded a major real estate consulting engagement with Warner Bros. Now, he was seeking a new growth opportunity—but not necessarily one with a young upstart.

Given Nick's background in real estate development, his entertainment industry relationships, his business school training, and Henry's strong endorsement, Nick seemed like the perfect candidate. So Rick and I converged on Los Angeles. We interviewed Nick, quickly moving from questions and qualifications to enthusiastically selling and recruiting. In an effort to secure Nick's commitment to lead the USI team on the West Coast, we formulated an offer, including performance-based equity. Nick eagerly accepted the challenge.

In short order, Nick developed an exclusive service relationship with Computer Science Corporation (CSC), which included strategic consulting, portfolio management, transaction management, and the development of a centralized property management system. Nick was very comfortable developing C-Suite relationships, cultivating warm business friendships with the CFO and the CAO of CSC. (See chapter 8, "Sales Is a Contact Sport," to learn how we landed this key account.)

Soon thereafter, Nick developed new account relationships with Farmers Insurance, DaVita Healthcare, Warner Bros., and Walt Disney in the Los Angeles Basin; Sutter Health in Sacramento; Charles Schwab and Toshiba in the San Francisco Bay Area; and Boeing and T-Mobile in Seattle. In five short years, we opened offices and grew our employee base in Sacramento, San Francisco, Seattle, Irvine, and Phoenix.

Nick routinely exceeded his West Region profit targets, achieved all of his equity performance goals, and eventually became the chief strategy officer of USI. Based on Nick's consistent performance, entrepreneurial spirit, and proven leadership skills, I felt confident expanding the scope of his responsibilities.

With Rick, Michael, and Nick in place, our new management team was organized to source, manage, and execute business throughout the United States. Investing in human growth catalysts is a vital step for every entrepreneur to fulfill their business vision.

## RELENTLESS PURSUIT OF GROWTH

Remember John Stanger's startup advice: "Do it! Do it! Do it!"

Invest in the three major growth catalysts: strategic leadership, product-line expansion, and geographic expansion. Find, recruit, and hire great people to plan, manage, and execute. Get out of their way and let them innovate.

Make sure that you take actions that will catapult your growth and enable your business to generate profits. These are the ones that worked for me:

- Open the door to new relationships.

- Monetize your business model.

- Turn preorders into contracts.

- Develop high-quality customer relationships.

- Invest in growth catalysts.

- Recruit and hire superior talent.

- Always pursue profitable growth.

# 7

## A HARD LESSON

The ideal formula for business success is when your passion and distinctive competence align. Only nine months after opening USI—a business based on my distinctive competence—I launched a second business called Sigma Communications Inc., or Sigma for short. Starting Sigma was the culmination of my long-standing passion to create a vehicle to more efficiently connect buyers and sellers of commercial real estate. The first product I envisioned was a high-quality commercial real estate magazine listing properties for sale, lease, and sublease. (Remember, in the early 1990s, the Internet was not yet widely available for commercial use.)

When I started Sigma, I believed that my passion for publishing the magazine would trump everything else. That proved to be a costly assumption. My Sigma venture is now a case study in why organizing a business based on your passion alone will substantially underperform a venture based on your distinctive competence.

Following your passion can lead you to make decisions fueled by fervor for your business idea instead of the knowledge and insight that comes with practical experience. I learned this firsthand. I lacked the experience, i.e., the distinctive competence, that I believe any new venture requires in its founder. I truly knew nothing about being a publisher. And my strong passion for becoming a publisher did not make up for that void. *This was Failure Point #1.*

## THE BIRTH OF SIGMA COMMUNICATIONS

Sigma's main purpose was to provide essential real estate information to the financial officers and real estate executives of the largest 5,000 companies in the United States through a single source. We set out to publish a high-quality, quarterly magazine, *The National Register of Commercial Real Estate*, to share ideas for dealing with surplus real estate and to efficiently link real estate buyers and sellers through the magazine's centerpiece, *The Commercial Property Exchange*. The Exchange would list surplus commercial property that was for sale, for lease, or for sublease.

When we started Sigma Communications, we thought we had all the pieces, but we were wrong.

## VALIDATING OUR CONCEPT

At the time we launched Sigma, the biggest issue facing financial officers and real estate executives was the surplus of commercial real estate in the United States. As we said in the Introduction, the collapse of hundreds of savings and loans (S&Ls) in 1989 had brought about the national financial slump of the early 1990s. As a result, capital was extremely scarce and interest rates were extraordinarily high. The nation was awash in unsold and unleased commercial properties. Malls and office buildings sat empty.

These circumstances made the market ripe for our business idea. We first tested our concept for *The Commercial Property Exchange* with a targeted group of the corporate real estate executives (CREs) of Fortune 100 companies. We also made a point to talk with insurance company executives because their companies had been the major underwriters of real estate development in the United States, and we knew they were anxious to unload their holdings.

Virtually all of the CREs we interviewed said they could use a central exchange of real estate listings. One CRE was particularly enthusiastic. "We need a vehicle to let buyers know what we have." With encouragement like that, we were convinced that Sigma was going to become a quick hit because it so clearly filled a need to make the market more efficient.

The problem was not validation but compensation. We confirmed interest in the magazine's concept, but we failed to ask our target audience to pay for the ads. As a result, we lost the opportunity to establish a paying customer base and generate an early revenue stream. This oversight cost us precious time and made our path to profitability that much more challenging. Looking back, I realize that our neglect to line up paying customers prior to launch was *Failure Point #2.*

## SIGMA'S VALUE PROPOSITION

Because there was no single published source for commercial real estate listings in the United States, CREs had no immediate way to identify available properties. This lack of information was a significant problem—a pain point—for companies when they needed to move offices or expand operations. At the same time, landlords and developers needed a more efficient way to attract buyers and lessees to their properties.

Our exchange would meet those needs. We felt that Sigma would provide the right vehicle to make the market more efficient by bringing buyers and sellers together. Listings and display ads would feature high-quality photographs and descriptions of properties. I was certain that our value proposition of "efficiently linking buyers and sellers" would be embraced immediately. In retrospect, it didn't matter what I thought about Sigma's value proposition—it only mattered how paying customers felt. This was *Failure Point #3*.

## Branding

Once we had validated our concept and solidified our value proposition, we took on branding. Like USI, we wanted our magazine to convey strength and substance. I was fond of the *duPont Registry*, which was (and still is) a well-respected buyer's guide to fine automobiles. We designed our magazine to have the same look and feel as the *duPont Registry*—heavy stock, full color, and glossy finish, with gold-embossed print on the cover.

We also wanted our new company's name and logo to be tied to USI as a complementary business. We took the corporate name, Sigma, from two sources: (1) The Greek letters for USI are upsilon, sigma, and iota, and (2) the mathematical symbol for sum is sigma. The centerpiece of our magazine, *The Commercial Property Exchange*, was going to be the only source for the *sum* total of all commercial real estate listings in the United States. To make the tie to USI even closer, I decided to make Sigma's logo consist of Greek letters upsilon, sigma, iota—*USI*.

Ultimately, the Sigma connection to USI did pay new client-development dividends—a point we will cover later.

**EFFICIENTLY LINKING BUYERS AND SELLERS**

SERVING FINANCIAL OFFICERS AND REAL ESTATE EXECUTIVES

Published Quarterly                                      Winter • 1993

# THE NATIONAL REGISTER
## OF
# COMMERCIAL
# REAL ESTATE

### NAFTA's Impact on Real Estate:

**United States:** Charles E. Roh, Assistant U.S. Trade Representative, North American Affairs
Joseph W. Duncan, Corporate Economist, Dun & Bradstreet

**Mexico:** Hermann von Bertrab, Director, NAFTA Office, Mexican Embassy
Jonathan Heath, General Manager, Macro Asesoría Económica

**Canada:** Michael Wilson, Minister for International Trade
Ruth Getter, Director, Economic Research, Toronto Dominion Bank

•

**"Earth In The Balance"**
Vice President Al Gore
Developer Melvin Simon

•

**Adjusting Investment Strategies**
MetLife's James B. Digney

•

**U.S. Bank Mega-Mergers**
BankAmerica • Chemical Bank • NationsBank

———

### The Commercial Property Exchange

*Cover of The National Register of Commercial Real Estate*

## SIGMA'S FUNDING

In addition to launching into what we thought was a highly receptive market, I felt the timing was right to self-fund. USI was generating plenty of profit. Since we kept careful control over our daily finances, I believed we could bootstrap Sigma with cash from USI.

Unfortunately, we had not properly factored the size and scale of Sigma, nor how long the ramp-up to profitability would take. Since I had never manufactured and shipped a product before, I underestimated the continuous cash drain from ongoing production and distribution.

If I had been organizing this business based on my distinctive competence, I would have understood the length of time and resources necessary, and I would have recognized the need for outside funding from the outset. I never would have bootstrapped. The funding decision was *Failure Point #4.*

## TRUSTED ADVISORS

Because I knew next to nothing about publishing a magazine, I needed guidance. Soon after we moved into USI's first office, we learned the Chairman Emeritus of Time Warner, Dick Munro, was in the neighboring space. I could not imagine a better advisor for our startup publication and decided to introduce myself. Since we had become friendly with his administrative assistant, I felt comfortable asking if I could meet with Dick.

As I walked down the hall for our initial meeting, I wondered if someone of his stature would take the time to speak to an entrepreneur new to publishing. It turned out that Dick was more than willing to open up to me. He listened carefully as I told him about my idea for my magazine. But I was surprised when he cautioned me that publications usually take a long time to become profitable.

"You've got very lofty goals," Dick said. "When we started *Sports Illustrated*, we didn't make a profit for six years. Are you prepared to wait that long?"

I assured Dick that we would do whatever was needed to make our journal successful. In the back of my mind, I had a different thought: We had launched USI and turned a profit in four months. Why couldn't we accomplish the same with Sigma? I was determined to beat the normal ramp-up to profitability in the publishing industry.

By the close of our discussion, Dick agreed to be our advisor. He immediately started reaching out to his network and introduced us to the publisher of *Garden Design* magazine. *Garden Design*'s publisher was amazingly friendly and generous with his time and knowledge.

As he took us through the mechanics of starting a publication, he, too, explained that publications take a long time to make money. First, we would need to build an audience. Then, we'd have to sell advertising space. He warned us that revenue from advertising would not start flowing immediately, and even then, it could be just a trickle for several years as we built our subscriber base.

*Garden Design*'s publisher was straightforward and very honest. He shared that publishing a magazine was an ongoing challenge. Achieving profitability was a constant struggle with progress measured in years, not months. Because I was used to moving at breakneck speed and expecting immediate returns, I felt we could outperform the publishing industry norm.

My unbridled passion for becoming a publisher, combined with my lack of distinctive competence, put blinders on me. I did not heed the advice of industry experts with superlative track records. Allowing my passion to overrun the common sense of listening to my advisors was *Failure Point #5.*

## RAMPING UP THE BUSINESS MODEL

Before we launched Sigma, we believed it would become bigger than USI. We invested to make our new publishing company run smoothly, attract advertisers, and grow. But launching Sigma was nothing like starting USI. We found ourselves on a monumental learning curve. Unfortunately, my enthusiasm blocked our team from the reality of obstacles in front of us.

To overcome our inexperience, we hired pieces of competence: an editor, a designer, and advertising sales people. We outsourced printing and distribution. I was the publisher but, ironically, the one person who lacked a core competence in publishing.

Our business model called for advertising sales in the form of commercial real estate listings, as well as traditional display ads. CFOs and CREs were the targets for soliciting paid listings for *The Commercial Property Exchange*. For the first time, a buyer in San Francisco could easily learn about a building for sale in New York without engaging a broker. Corporations with headquarters in Atlanta could discover properties on the market in Denver without flying to the market.

With the huge number of commercial properties available, we figured we'd be raking in the advertising dollars very quickly. As it turned out, this assumption was dead wrong. Even a market flooded with surplus property needed time to adjust to a new way of doing business. Not allowing enough time for the market to transition to a new, disruptive model was *Failure Point #6*.

### Preview Issue

We launched by publishing a preview issue with sample listings in the summer of 1992 and sent it out to 20,000 CFOs and CREs. We used the sample listings to demonstrate the quality and usefulness of our advertising formats.

We created compelling content to heighten reader interest, give the magazine cachet, and enhance sales of display ads. The preview issue included survey results from the top 100 corporate real estate executives highlighting their most important challenges. The survey showed that dealing with surplus real estate was their number one problem. We also included interviews with CREs discussing success stories, as well as a piece featuring service providers—including USI. This was the first step of the Sigma/USI co-marketing strategy, as you will read in "The Trojan Horse" later in this chapter.

The preview issue clearly demonstrated that our magazine offered a new way to solve the surplus real estate problem by more efficiently linking buyers and sellers.

## Operations

Once the preview issue was out, we had to produce our first regular issue. Our editor worked with us to sculpt the stories we wrote and helped us hire journalists to conduct the interviews. Our designer laid out the graphical look of the magazine and educated us on the details of getting our journal ready for printing. Because we were so intent on making a high-quality product, we got deeply into the details of picking the paper, deciding on the quality of printing, and overseeing the production runs. We approved every page of the book prior to sending it to the printer.

Our printer helped us understand how the editorial copy and the ads would come together in a press run. They also handled the mailing. We learned quickly that efficient order fulfillment is crucial to the success of any manufacturing business. And make no mistake, we were manufacturing a product.

While we were excited to be publishing a high-quality magazine, the work was overwhelming. To manage our operations, we produced a master schedule to organize and coordinate our tasks to get the product out on time and at the quality level our customers expected. The first month of each quarter was devoted to editorial. The second month was for design and production. And the third month was all printing, publishing, and shipping. Of course, commercial listings were updated continuously.

Shipping wasn't all that easy. We found that we had to modify and upgrade the mailing list of 20,000 recipients before each printing, which was a very expensive, time-consuming process. There was no point mailing an expensive magazine to people no longer in their positions. Nowadays, if you're distributing information via email, you'll need to update your list regularly to add willing readers and to remove bad addresses and people who have opted out of your mailings.

## BEST LAID PLANS

After almost two years and six issues, things started to become stressful. Our business model was not working as planned. Advertising revenues were slow to trickle in. While some major holders of real estate agreed to place listings, many did not. The deep recession in commercial real estate had forced corporations to freeze all marketing budgets. Many of the big real estate holders were not allowed to spend a dime on advertising, even though corporations were spending millions just to maintain their surplus real estate.

Selling display advertising to premium advertisers also proved to be extremely challenging. As a new publication, we did not have an audited circulation. While we wanted to sell a full-page, four-color ad for $10,000, no advertisers would pay that amount. We were lucky to get $5,000 for a four-color ad and $2,500 for a black-and-white ad. When we approached big advertisers like Absolut Vodka, they said they would love to put an ad in our magazine, but they would not pay us anything for the placement because we had no way to prove the size of our circulation.

With little advertising revenue flowing in, we had to rely on USI's profits to fund most of Sigma's cash needs. To make matters worse, we found ourselves spending 80 percent of our time on Sigma and only 20 percent on our cash cow, USI.

By its third year, Sigma was still burning cash. Quarterly advertising revenue was averaging $100,000 per issue, while expenses were running at $200,000 per issue (20,000 copies × $10 per copy = $200,000 in expenses). We were losing $100,000 per issue and could not forecast when we would break even. We started to hit a wall.

Dick Munro was right. Generating a profit from a publication was a slow process. We were taking the cash USI was generating and using it to fund Sigma, which had begun to run an annual deficit of $400,000. We could not continue to bleed cash and rely on USI for funds. USI needed money to fund its own growth. If we had planned properly, we would have raised funding to see us through the six years it typically takes for a national publication to become profitable. Because the business did not work as we expected, we did not have the resources—time, money, and expertise—to work through the changes that were needed. Having insufficient resources was *Failure Point #7*.

## THE TROJAN HORSE

Even though *The National Register of Commercial Real Estate* was a cash sink, it did pay off in other ways. The magazine began to act as a Trojan horse for USI. We ran USI ads and included interviews and articles about our outsourcing model for corporate real estate. We also used Sigma's extensive, targeted mailing list to create a direct-mail marketing campaign for USI. With copies landing quarterly on the desks of 20,000 real estate professionals, the journal continually raised awareness of USI.

We soon found that influential real estate executives welcomed us into their offices. We discovered that top executives were eager to be interviewed for our magazine and have their pictures taken. The interviews served as a lucrative entrée to introduce USI's real estate services. As we talked with more real estate owners, investors, and service providers, the interviews also became a tool for competitive analysis.

In interviews, our competitors candidly told us about their business, discounting the magazine's connection to USI. Sigma, with its glossy magazine, looked much bigger, more prosperous, and more influential than it actually was. Our magazine became the Trojan horse that gave USI exposure to 20,000 CFOs and CREs of the largest corporations, all while flying under the radar of our competitors.

If it hadn't been for the symbiotic relationship between USI and Sigma, with USI funding Sigma, and Sigma serving as a marketing arm for USI, we never would have been able to keep the publishing company going as long as we did.

## A BANKABLE BUSINESS MODEL?

Given the situation, I began to weigh the pros and cons of keeping Sigma Communications alive. Even though Dick Munro had told us it took *Sports Illustrated* six years to make a profit, and even though Sigma was opening doors for USI to gain new customers, I was becoming impatient. The cash, the time, and the brainpower Sigma was absorbing were becoming more and more frustrating.

As countless publishers and online businesses have discovered, creating useful content, and then making money from it through subscriptions, advertising, and fees, do not always add up to a bankable business model. And without direct experience in publishing, it was very hard for us to figure out how to modify our model to put Sigma on a faster path to profitability. We were puzzled. Why wasn't the corporate real estate market willing to pay for a more efficient way to connect buyer and seller?

When Bloomberg asked to include *The Commercial Property Exchange* as a part of their financial information services, we were tempted to keep Sigma going. As a last-ditch effort, we made a deal with Bloomberg to include our property listings on their terminals. All you had to do was type "CPE Go" to get to our proprietary information. But even with growth drivers like Bloomberg, we still couldn't reach breakeven.

We evaluated every possible way to save money from operations without compromising quality. We even factored in the benefits Sigma delivered to USI in terms of marketing and gaining entrées to new lucrative customers. We did long-term financial projections to understand how much funding we needed to keep our doors open. When we finally considered seeking outside funding, we were just too late. We had run out of gas.

## SEVEN FAILURE POINTS

Looking back, I realize that we made seven crucial errors:

1. I had no competence, experience, or track record in publishing.

2. I did not secure preorders to validate the business model.

3. I let my passion blind me to the realities of the market.

4. I did not plan adequate funding for the scope of the venture.

5. I did not listen to the advice of advisors and industry experts.

6. I did not budget adequate time to sell a new business model.

7. I did not have sufficient resources to reach profitability.

## CLOSING THE BUSINESS

No one wants to kill their own business. But I was a capitalist and a pragmatist at heart and realized the time had come to part ways with Sigma. To me, the purpose of a business is to generate a profit. After three intensive years, with a quarterly cash drain of over $100,000, I decided it was time to pull the plug.

We finally acknowledged that the business model for Sigma had limitations and would continue to struggle with cash flow. We realized our productivity was suffering from a split focus. Looking back, I now know that Sigma's main business was manufacturing a product—not just creating a source of information to bring buyers and sellers together. Producing inventory and shipping it out on a regular basis—even in the form of a magazine—required a constant flow of cash and countless hours of direct and indirect manpower. This was not a model I was used to managing. My expertise lay in running a service business.

Our attorney helped us unwind Sigma. He made sure we addressed all of our legal obligations. We had to advise our customers that we would be shutting Sigma down. In some cases we had to issue refunds. We also needed to inform our suppliers and make sure that all of our contracts and commitments were fulfilled, including payment of outstanding invoices. Our staff had served the Sigma mission with total dedication. Since USI was growing, we offered Sigma employees jobs at USI.

Starting Sigma had been the culmination of a long-term vision to create a vehicle that would more efficiently connect buyers and sellers of commercial real estate. In the end analysis, my passion for this project could not overcome my lack of distinctive competence. The hardest lesson I learned from the Sigma experience is this:

*Don't just follow your passion. Follow your expertise.*

Expertise is not as sexy and exciting as passion. But starting a business in which you have distinctive competence will give you a much greater chance of being successful.

## Learning from Failure

- Don't confuse a passion project with building a business around your distinctive competence.

- Before launching, line up preorders. Early sales provide vital proof you are on the right track.

- Don't let your passion blind you to the realities of your market.

- Make sure you have the resources to succeed: time, money, and expertise.

- Pay attention and listen to the advice of trusted advisors.

- Be pragmatic and evaluate all the costs and benefits of staying in business.

- Know when to fold. Sometimes accepting reality and learning from failure is the best option.

SECTION

# 3

—

# GROWTH STAGE

# 8

## SALES IS A CONTACT SPORT

USI had a highly productive sales force. For many years, we enjoyed a 50 percent close rate on qualified prospects. We honed our value proposition, organized for battle, and relentlessly pursued every target as though our lives depended on it. There was a point when one of our competitors exclaimed, "USI seems to win every time." Building an effective sales force is vital to every organization that has a product or service that requires face-to-face contact with the customer to secure an order.

USI was a *multimillion-dollar* upstart in the real estate outsourcing space surrounded by *multibillion-dollar* competitors including CBRE, Jones Lang LaSalle, and Cushman & Wakefield. But we did win more than our fair share of new business because we were highly selective in recruiting and investing in the very best salespeople to obtain the very best results.

Like high-performance athletes, we developed a mind-set that we deserved to win every time we competed. We described our competitive drive by coining the phrase *Sales is a contact sport*. It made no difference whether male or female; it was all about the attitude and the commitment to win.

## THE HAIL MARY

Probably the best way that I can describe USI's mind-set about winning is to share how we overcame a gut-wrenching sales experience. Nick Westley, USI's Western Region executive, and I had been working for over a year in pursuit of Computer Science Corporation's (CSC) real estate business. Landing this business would have a dramatic impact on our company's bottom line.

After joining USI in 1996, Nick's first sales call was on Computer Science Corporation. USI's West Coast office and CSC's corporate headquarters were both in El Segundo, California. Over the next 18 months, Nick cultivated a very strong C-Suite relationship with CSC's chief financial officer, Lee Level, and chief administrative officer Tom Newman. At the same time, we developed a relationship with Terry Bilbo, CSC's director of corporate administration in Fairfax, Virginia. Terry was responsible for real estate and facilities, among other duties, and had offices on both coasts.

Besides real estate, Terry and I shared a common interest in the Dallas Cowboys. He even had a football signed by Roger Staubach on his desk. You couldn't be a Cowboy fan without loving Roger—better known as "Captain Comeback." Every Cowboys fan knew that prior to playing for the Cowboys, Roger had won the Heisman Trophy while playing college ball at Navy.

Although Terry and I had a shared devotion to the Cowboys, Roger represented a real risk to USI in the business world. When Roger retired from the NFL, he started a commercial real estate brokerage firm, The Staubach Company, which had grown over the years into a national powerhouse. Even though our business models were different, both Nick and I knew we had to watch out for Staubach as a potential competitor.

Finally, CSC decided to issue a request for proposal (RFP) for the outsourcing of their real estate services. Nick and the whole USI team poured endless hours into a highly detailed and tailored proposal. Besides providing a full suite of services through a dedicated on-site team, we quantified the opportunity to save $35 million for CSC. We had strong indications that we were the frontrunner in the competition for CSC's business. Nonetheless, we continued to nurture all of our relationships with the CSC executive team.

Early in the week of the contract award, we received feedback that USI had the inside track. Then, out of the blue on Friday, Terry called Nick to advise him that The Staubach Company had won the bid. We were stunned. Corporate real estate outsourcing was not Staubach's core business. Nick and I were beside ourselves. We could not accept the news. So Nick called Lee Level and Tom Newman to request a meeting for Monday.

To make matters worse, it was the weekend of the annual Army–Navy football game. I couldn't get the image out of my head that Terry and Roger were probably sharing a hot dog on the Navy sidelines. It bothered me so much that I called Nick to say I was joining him in California to repackage our proposal on Sunday in preparation for the last-ditch effort on Monday.

We knew we needed a head-snapper—USI parlance for a dramatic differentiator. Nick and I felt so confident about our value proposition that we decided to offer an advance payment of $1 million against the $35 million savings goal. We figured a $1 million Hail Mary check up front could overcome whatever Captain Comeback had to offer.

Nick and I met with Lee and Tom in El Segundo while Terry dialed in from Fairfax. When we recounted our relationship history, presented our value proposition, and committed the $1 million advance on the savings promise; Lee, Tom, and Terry agreed that USI should win the bid. The Hail Mary check had an impact, but the C-Suite relationship that Nick had developed was what really won the day.

## THE CONTACT-SPORT MIND-SET

Let's delve deeper into the mind-set that sales is a contact sport. Not everyone likes contact sports. Not everyone is good at contact sports. Contact sports are physical, direct, and active. You need to be highly competitive, thick-skinned, and productive in your position. You can get hurt playing contact sports. There is a winner, and there is a loser. The better you execute your role, the more likely your team will win.

Deciding to try out and participate in contact sports is a choice. When you make that choice, you are agreeing to fulfill a role, a responsibility, and a duty to your team. You may make the team, or you may get cut. Most contact sports require extensive coaching, preparation, training, special equipment, and a well-developed game plan including advanced strategy and tactics. Contact sports require investment of time, money, and skill development. The best athletes expect to win every time. When the best athletes do not win, they suffer, but they apply what they have learned to the next contest.

Building an effective sales force is expensive and time-consuming. There are no shortcuts. Choose your team carefully. If you fill your roster with second-rate talent, you should expect second-rate results. Since your sales force is the face of the organization to the customer, it is imperative to be highly selective and recognize that selling embodies many of the characteristics of contact sports.

## THIS PRODUCT IS SO INNOVATIVE, IT WILL SELL ITSELF!

Before we discuss the process of building a sales team, let's take a step back and talk about the two vital roles that contribute to an organization's success. Internal producers *develop* products, and external producers *sell* products. The required skill sets are both essential, but different.

Capable product developers are steeped in hard skills, which include design, engineering, production, manufacturing, and distribution. On the other hand, effective product sellers have an abundance of soft skills including strategizing, proposing, influencing, qualifying, selling, and closing. As the business leader, you need to make sure that your organization includes a balance of each type of producer. Many times we hear of entrepreneurs who develop new products and exclaim, "This product is so innovative, it will sell itself!" The road to the entrepreneur's graveyard is paved with the remains of businesses that held this belief.

Products do not build themselves, and products do not sell themselves. You need internal producers to build your products, and you need external producers—or salespeople—to lead the charge in selling your products.

## BUILDING YOUR SALES FORCE

Prior to forming USI, I had spent my entire career in sales and marketing roles. I recognized that building an effective sales force was vital to achieving USI's long-term growth. In the early years, I was focused on hiring the best available "athlete" on a very limited budget. All of our training was trial by fire, and everyone had the responsibility to sell. As the business grew, we implemented a formal development plan to build our sales force that included all of the following components:

1. Creating a profit-based reward structure

2. Forming geographic coverage plans

3. Developing recruiting and hiring plans

4. Conducting product and sales training

5. Setting sales goals and quotas

6. Developing sales aids

7. Understanding sales as a process

8. Selling by customer referrals

### NOTE

The remainder of this chapter provides a detailed explanation of each of the eight components recommended to build your sales force.

## Creating a Profit-Based Reward Structure

The single most important recommendation that I can make to entrepreneurs to ensure a profitable business is to reward your sales force with a percentage of profits—not revenues—on their accounts.

This is a surefire way to turn your sales force into P&L managers for each of their accounts. Think about it. Since salespeople are concerned about maximizing their personal income, then why not set up a system that maximizes the business income at the same time?

It amazes me to think of the number of businesses that reward their sales force with a percentage of revenue—sometimes paying out more than 50 percent of gross sales. I believe this is a prescription for failure—especially for small to medium-size businesses. A revenue-based reward structure may work well when times are good, but it can cause your business to suffer when times are bad.

You should hire the best salespeople to be your face to the customer. Then utilize their sales skills to bring in the business, and the profit incentive to ensure financial performance. Of course, you will need to establish guidelines to achieve your desired profit goals.

Most sales compensation models are organized to reset quota and compensation every year, whereas a profit-based reward system pays a percentage of profit and continues to do so for the life of the account. A successful salesperson can build an annuity that will continue to grow over time as new accounts are added and existing accounts are expanded. If you think about it, each year builds on the prior year, creating tremendous incentive for each salesperson to retain accounts, expand accounts, and add new accounts. Compensation is compounded, so your sales force has a vested interest to stay with the company and help it grow.

For example, at USI we compensated our sales force with a base salary plus a 10 percent profits interest on all their existing accounts, new accounts, and new product-line sales. Unlike other sales organizations, USI paid its sales force a profits interest for the life of the account. This motivated the sales force to be active P&L managers concerned about account growth, retention, renewal, and full optimization of all our service lines. As the compensation compounded, it created greater incentive to stay and grow with USI. As a result, sales force turnover was exceedingly low—less than five percent each year.

## Forming Geographic Coverage Plans

Distributing your sales force to optimize geographic coverage hinges on your understanding and location of the ideal customer. The ideal customer is defined as the perfect buyer for your product. The perfect buyer believes your product will resolve their pain, and they have the budget, the authority, and the motivation to buy it.

Before we discuss the parameters for defining your ideal customer, we should take a step back to reflect on the development of your value proposition. As covered in chapter 3, "Dynamic Planning," we posed the following questions to help you validate and flesh out your value proposition:

- Does your customer have substantial unserved needs— pain points?

- Does your product address your customer's unserved needs—does it resolve the pain?

- How much does the unserved need cost your customer— what is the cost of ongoing pain?

- How does your customer benefit from your product— what is the value of pain relief?

- Is your customer motivated to buy your product repeatedly—does it prevent recurring pain?

- Does your product serve a large and growing market— are there lots of customers in pain?

- Do you have a sustainable competitive advantage— do you have a unique solution to the pain?

With a clear understanding of your value proposition, you are ready to define your ideal customer by answering the following questions:

- What are your ideal customer's top three pain points?

- In which industries does your ideal customer operate?

- Where is your ideal customer located (geographical factors)?

- What is the size of your ideal customer's company?

- What is the title and role of your ideal customer?

- How many ideal customers are there (number of buyers)?

- When does your ideal customer buy (seasonality)?

- How does your ideal customer buy (procurement)?

- Does your ideal customer control the budget?

- How does your ideal customer achieve career success?

The answers to these questions will help you develop optimal coverage plans—the ratio of salespeople to ideal customers by geographic area. By effectively allocating and managing sales personnel, you will be able to maximize your existing sales force productivity and map out additional recruiting needs.

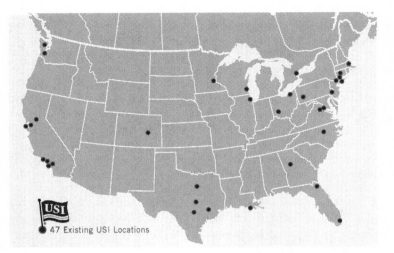

*USI Geographic Coverage Map*

## Developing Recruiting and Hiring Plans

Your geographic coverage map will identify gaps in your sales force that will guide your recruiting and hiring plans. Similar to a professional sports draft, you will have a priority list of the positions you need to fill—only adjusting for the opportunity to recruit and land a superstar talent (like LeBron James, for example), even if it means hiring that person out of sequence with your market needs.

For the most part, USI recruited against a geographic plan, but on a few occasions, we veered from our plans in order to draft or promote a truly unique talent. Tricia Shay comes to mind as a unique draft choice. She was originally hired as a database administrator but so consistently overperformed her duties in operations that she was promoted repeatedly into business development and P&L management roles, ultimately becoming a partner in the business. Likewise, as referenced in chapter 6, "Do It! Do It! Do It!," we veered sharply from our plan in order to recruit Rick Bertasi. His impact on sales and operations earned him the title of President and made him the second-largest shareholder.

### Assessing and Interviewing

As USI grew and we ramped up business development, we needed to step back to assess the performance of our sales team. Some had stellar track records, while others underperformed. We analyzed both the work requirements for sales and the characteristics of the producers who exceeded those requirements. We also studied the traits of people who did not achieve their business development goals.

As we boiled down the work requirements for sales, we learned that successful producers performed favorably against the following criteria:

- Eager to perform alone in the field
- Competent in questioning, listening, and note taking
- Comfortable influencing the way customers think
- Able to create new ways to resolve problems
- Willing to hold out new ideas to be accepted or rejected
- Capable of translating ideas into profitable proposals
- Disciplined in following up and closing repeatedly

After analysis, we realized USI's high performers had the following characteristics:

- Thrived on competition and valued discipline
- Possessed an overwhelming desire to win
- Routinely invested in preparation
- Enjoyed tailoring solutions to fit needs
- Wanted to be measured on their results
- Performed well in high-pressure situations
- Responded to performance-based compensation
- Regularly overperformed assigned sales goals

These criteria and characteristics became the basis for hiring USI sales personnel. We developed an exhaustive interview process for weeding out the pretenders from the genuine producers. USI did not utilize its human resources department to qualify sales professionals. Only P&L managers with direct sales responsibility interviewed and short-listed sales candidates. No sales producers were hired without having interviewed with at least five USI P&L managers. Frankly, the interview process was so intense that the pretenders would often pull themselves out of the running when they realized there would be no place for them to hide at USI.

USI's sales force played a key role in achieving our 40 percent compounded annual growth rate. We had no room or tolerance for non-producers. I strongly recommend that you develop strict disciplines for hiring and recruiting your sales force. Having a highly productive sales force is one of the best ways to scale your business. A strong sales force will enable you to open new markets, find new customers, expand existing relationships, and produce vital cash flow for sustainable growth.

## Conducting Sales Training

Having completed both IBM's and HP's formal sales training programs, I had a strong appreciation for the importance of high-quality training on sales force productivity.

When I joined IBM straight out of college, the company was recognized for teaching the "IBM Way" to all its newly hired salespeople. IBM taught me how to sell—everything from planning a successful sales call to making an effective presentation. I learned how to identify the need, conceptualize the solution, qualify the customer, and cost-justify the proposal. IBM trained me to quantify the value proposition, handle objections, and close the order. Beyond the emblematic white shirts, blue suits, and wing tips, IBM also taught important lessons about competing fairly and not disparaging the competition—essential principles for success.

Later at HP, I went through advanced sales training, attending Miller-Heiman Strategic Selling. The lessons from Strategic Selling had a significant impact on my sales performance. HP was so committed to the program that they sent a group of us to become certified Strategic Selling trainers. Miller-Heiman's sales training was, and still is, one of the best sales training programs available.

### Applying Sales Lessons at USI

During our startup years, I made sure we applied what I had learned at IBM and HP to selling at USI. Our early training consisted of a mentorship program. We paired new hires with experienced members of our sales force to bring the new salespeople up to speed on USI's selling process.

As we hit our growth phase, we needed experienced producers more quickly than a mentoring program could accommodate. As a result, we decided to hire only professional salespeople. Even though our new hires were experienced, they still needed training on USI's profit model and value proposition. To address this need, we developed a competitive six-month training program built around a comprehensive business case that required the participants to do the following:

- Work in cross-functional teams
- Apply advanced product knowledge
- Make practice sales calls and deliver pitches
- Develop business cases and profit models
- Generate comprehensive proposals
- Present the value proposition to a formal board
- Address objections and close for the order

In addition to meeting at regular intervals throughout the year, we assembled all training program members in a central off-site location to make final presentations to USI senior partners—delivering the pitch, presenting the value proposition, answering questions, dealing with objections, and closing the sale.

As USI matured, we invested in advanced sales training with Miller-Heiman. I had chosen this particular brand of training because it had been so beneficial to me. Strategic Selling fit like a glove with our professional sales force.

A young company with a complex product that requires a dedicated sales force will always be challenged with the decision to buy or build the sales talent. Like most small, high-growth businesses, we decided to hire a professional sales force and only provide advanced product and sales training.

## Setting Sales Goals and Quotas

Our method for setting sales goals wasn't very sophisticated during our startup years. We were focused on generating enough sales revenue to cover our costs, make a profit, and fund our growth.

As USI started to mature, Rick Bertasi led the charge in developing a formal sales plan, which included the establishment of sales quotas. At the beginning of each new fiscal year, we would assign sales goals, and then we would challenge each producer to come up with a plan to achieve them. Once the individual plans were developed, we would meet as a group at a central location for a three-day campout. We dissected the numbers and reworked sales quotas based on four factors: sales performance record, new account procurement, qualified prospects in the funnel, and ability to sell additional services to the existing customer base.

As you can imagine, these three-day in-your-face marathons got pretty intense. Everyone was challenged to overachieve—sometimes to the point of extreme discomfort. We didn't pull any punches. Of course, we always ended these sessions as teammates committed to goal achievement, fighting side by side in the trenches—but it wasn't always pretty getting there.

Rick and I had differing points of view on establishing individual sales goals. I was of the mind that sales quotas should be achievable, leaving room for the producer to overperform, whereas Rick would assign "stretch goals," requiring each producer to overperform just to meet 100 percent of their goal. Rick believed that top-performing competitors would find a way to win. In the end, we struck a balance.

## Developing Sales Aids

As soon as goals are set, your sales force will begin to engage the market. Naturally, they will be seeking tools that convey your message and motivate the customer to buy. Providing your sales force with a well-developed set of sales aids will ensure a consistent message about your business. The key word is *consistent*. In many respects, a set of well-developed sales aids should magnify your voice as the business leader.

Since your voice is limited to people within your reach, and a growing organization requires consistent messaging to many customers in many places at many different times, a standard set of sales aids can play a vital role in building the brand and expanding the business. An initial set of sales aids should clarify the business purpose, explain the value proposition, and emphasize competitive advantage. As the business leader, you should play an active role in developing and approving sales aids.

If you do not provide a uniform set of sales aids to your team, they will develop their own. In one sense, you want team members to take the initiative and be creative. On the other hand, you run the risk of confusing the customer and the market with differing messages. I believe that consistency should take priority. Of course, every team member can always develop and recommend new ways to communicate the message. But you should retain central control over the message—especially during business liftoff.

Having spent most of my career in sales and marketing, I have found that the single most effective sales aid is the One-Voice

Presentation. A One-Voice Presentation is a uniform set of information that reinforces key messages about your business, its purpose, and the value proposition—with absolute consistency. A One-Voice Presentation makes it crystal clear to all team members the importance of communicating a common message to the customer.

In addition to the One-Voice Presentation, here is a list of sales aids that will reinforce your message, increase sales force productivity, and support new business sales:

- Business purpose infographic
- Value proposition presentation deck
- Product features & benefits e-documents
- Customer testimonial ads
- Competitive advantage infographic
- Proposal and financial template
- Standardized customer contract

A limited marketing budget can go a long way if you take the time to develop uniform sales aids that communicate a consistent message. Utilizing all forms of electronic media to distribute your sales aids is the most efficient way to put these tools in the hands of your sales force and in front of your customer.

## Understanding Sales as a Process

Too often selling is perceived as a single customer encounter ending with a simple yes or no answer. It is convenient to think that all the salesperson needs to do is place a phone call to line up a meeting and ask for the order. Nothing about selling could be further from the truth.

In reality, selling is a process made up of a series of customer encounters that include successive decisions to buy in. Selling is complex, time consuming, and fraught with uncertainty.

Selling is complex because it involves numerous engagements, requiring increasing levels of preparation, and taking place over a significant block of time. This block of time is commonly referred to as the sales cycle, or the time it takes from initial engagement to closing the sale. Each product or service has a different sales cycle. For example, USI's outsourcing proposition had a nine-month sales cycle.

Selling is time consuming because it involves a sequence of well-prepared steps including sales calls, presentations, seminars, conferences, tailored proposals, reference checks, executive approvals, contract negotiations, and final closing.

## THE SALES PROCESS

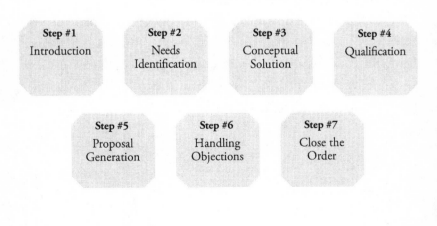

Selling is uncertain because of the unknowns impacting the buyer. These unknowns can increase or decrease the potential to close a deal, or cost you time in pursuing a dead end. The only way to mitigate this risk is to continually qualify the buyer throughout the selling process. Qualifying is a vital skill because it protects time—a salesperson's greatest asset. Qualifying can be uncomfortable but it heightens respect and mutual accountability with your buyer.

## The Sales Pitch

The sales process starts with a direct engagement with your prospect. One of the best ways to make a lasting first impression is to deliver an effective sales pitch.

Every time you are asked about your business, you are given the opportunity to make a pitch. This is your chance to create excitement about your business, establish your brand, and secure a new customer. Each time you speak about your business, you are either making a connection or missing a connection. Invest the time to practice your sales pitch and get it right.

In many respects, your sales pitch is a high-level summary of your value proposition. As long as you have confidence in your value proposition, your only challenge is to keep your pitch concise. Your pitch should include all of the following components:

- Brief introduction: highlights your credentials and establishes you as the expert

- Business purpose: states the customer problem and provides an overview of the solution

- Value creation: demonstrates how the customer will benefit and how you will alleviate the customer's pain

- Customer promise: defines how the customer will realize genuine, measurable value

- Engagement request: continues the selling process by documenting the agreed follow-up action plan

The classic "elevator pitch" is the 30-second version of your sales pitch; it clearly communicates the pain point, the solution, and the promise. The elevator pitch must be so compelling that it earns you the right to request and secure a dedicated meeting. Once again, practice makes perfect.

An effective sales pitch will earn you the right to start making sales calls, laying the foundation for a successful close.

## The Sales Call

Selling is expensive. You have to spend money on preparation and travel to get face-to-face with potential customers. In this world of emails and social media, we sometimes forget how valuable it is to sit down with someone in person. Social media and email campaigns can serve to keep you and your business top of mind for a customer but usually cannot replace a personal sales call.

In a nutshell, here are the steps required for executing a successful sales call:

1. Make the introduction.

    a. Introduce yourself, your background, your role, and the purpose of the meeting.

    **b.** Inquire about your customer, their background, their role, and their goals for the meeting.

    **c.** Engage by finding common ground on a personal and a business level.

**2.** Assess business needs.

    **a.** Ask probing questions to learn about pain points.

    **b.** Generate a list of concerns and pain points.

    **c.** Begin to link pain points to value proposition.

**3.** Develop conceptual solution.

    **a.** Brainstorm solution framework.

    **b.** Connect macro-solution components to pain points.

    **c.** Confirm interest and commitment to proceed.

    **d.** Qualify approval process, budget, and time frame.

**4.** Sell features, advantages, and benefits.

    **a.** Connect product features and benefits to needs.

    **b.** Flesh out major features, advantages, and benefits.

    **c.** Explain how product resolves pain.

    **d.** Summarize unique benefits of proposed solution.

**5.** Quantify value proposition.

    **a.** Develop cost/benefit summary.

    **b.** Quantify resource requirements and time frames.

    **c.** Present case studies to demonstrate value proposition.

    **d.** Re-qualify approval process, budget, and time frame.

**6.** Summarize economic model including costs, benefits, resources, and time frames.

7. Handle objections and close.

    a. Agree on goals and next process steps.

    b. Identify additional decision makers.

    c. Secure commitment for additional information.

    d. Close for appropriate commitment.

## THE IMPACT OF CUSTOMER TESTIMONIALS

Utilizing a customer referral is the best way to secure new business. Connecting your prospect with an established customer opens a direct pipeline for an honest dialogue about the strengths and weaknesses of your proposal. A satisfied customer can say things about your product that you can only dream about saying. There are no conflicts. Potential concerns around trust can be neutralized. A strong customer testimonial can compress the sales cycle, making it easier to close the order.

During our startup years, USI was fortunate to nurture customer testimonials from Patterson Dental and IDS/American Express. Referrals from Patterson and IDS played a significant role in USI's early growth. These testimonials and case studies were valuable weapons in our sales arsenal.

As USI's business matured, the majority of our new business sales came from customer referrals. Our customer testimonials were so effective that we decided to develop a series of ads featuring client CFOs and CREs. Each ad pictured an executive discussing the hard savings they realized from USI's outsourcing solution.

A CFO reference from a major corporation can have a direct and certain impact, oftentimes turning your prospects into paying customers. Our ad featuring Ron Zappile, President of United

Technologies Realty, proclaimed, "A Partnership that has saved $42 Million in 24 months."

*USI testimonial ad in* CFO *magazine*

This testimonial campaign was our biggest single contributor to new account development. The ads ran in *CFO* magazine and were reproduced for use as sales aids. Almost 80 percent of our new sales came from referrals and testimonials from our existing client base.

## EVERYBODY SELLS

The responsibility to win new business went well beyond the direct sales force. Everyone on the USI team had the obligation to sell; even our backroom staff had the incentive to make introductions. We rewarded anyone who played a role in the selling process, from sharing leads and referrals to participating in a sales call to actually helping to close a deal. If an administrative assistant introduced a field salesperson to a good lead, he or she earned a share in the financial success. The greater the role an employee played, the greater the financial reward.

Building your sales force will take a dedicated investment of time, talent, and money. The returns will propel your growth and enable you to realize your business vision. I recommend you consider taking these steps in building your sales force:

1. Create a profit-based reward structure.

2. Configure geographic coverage plans.

3. Develop recruiting and hiring plans.

4. Conduct product and sales training.

5. Set sales goals and quotas.

6. Develop sales aids.

7. Manage sales as a process.

8. Sell by customer referral.

9. You just might build a different sales force if you adopt the view that *sales is a contact sport.*

# 9

## THE TEN COMMANDMENTS
## OF STARTUP PROFIT

Even with a 40 percent compounded annual growth rate, USI's consistent success was overshadowed by the dot-com boom in 1999. USI was the tortoise, and the promise of the Internet was the hare. It seemed that everyone was jumping on the Internet bandwagon to ride the electronic superhighway to untold fortune and fame. Every day, new businesses were being formed and funded with only a name, a concept, and the promise of future revenues. There were literally thousands of new dot-com businesses being introduced to the market on a wing and a prayer.

Some of these businesses went public in an investor feeding frenzy that drove stock prices to exponential multiples of revenue. Many of these businesses had never even made a profit. It seemed that everyone was required to bet on the come. Employee compensation was based on stock options and ultra-low salaries in exchange for the promise to work 24 hours a day, seven days a week.

Although somewhat envious of the paper wealth created, I felt certain that it was going to come apart at the seams. How could a concept business with minimal revenue, very few contracts, disproportional budgets, undisciplined spending, and no profits in the offing survive? It seemed like a house of cards just waiting for the wind to pick up.

Mind you, it's not that I don't like tech startups; I do. It's just that there were literally hundreds of new dot-com businesses being formed, without much differentiation, in the narrowest of vertical markets. Each of these new businesses was in hot pursuit of customers, striving to take the high ground and become the industry standard without enough capital to stay afloat. Of course, there were exceptions.

USI was not a sexy dot-com being pursued by investment bankers to make a public offering, even though our numbers were robust. We were generating a 20 percent operating profit and funding expansion from free cash flow. The dichotomy was remarkable. Tried-and-true businesses that made consistent profits were passed over for unproven dot-com models with no track record. It made no sense to me. (Nowadays, investors are more selective about the product, the team, and the real opportunity to capture users and become a dominant player in its market.)

The operating model during the dot-com boom was the antithesis of USI's structured approach to making money. The eventual dot-com collapse validated the benefits of operating disciplines and financial controls on the production of genuine profits. It crystallized my belief that the purpose of every business is profit.

From the beginning, USI was organized around 10 core profit principles. I call these profit principles *The Ten Commandments of Startup Profit*. We factored profit into every business decision that we made. The 10 profit principles listed below get at the nub of how USI made consistent profits and how they can help you build an enduring business that produces sustainable profits as well.

## THE TEN COMMANDMENTS OF STARTUP PROFIT

In many respects, the following principles are discussed to differing levels and degrees throughout this book. This concentrated list of profit principles can be used to benchmark your business model and its potential for generating profit.

1. Build a Business Based on Your Distinctive Competence.

2. Develop and Deliver a Superior Value Proposition.

3. Don't Start Up Until . . .

   a. You know how you're going to generate revenue

   b. You know how much it will cost to run your business

   c. You know how you're going to make a profit

   d. You have preorders to validate your business model and liftoff plans

   e. You have lined up the funding you need to reach breakeven

   f. You understand the impact of startup funding on cost and control

4. Take Charge of the Money and Control It.

5. Create a Profit-Based Reward Structure.

6. Recognize and Hire "Lightning in a Bottle."

7. Create Profit Centers to Scale Your Business.

8. Augment Profits with Proprietary Applications.

9. Build a Financial War Chest for Strategic Advantage.

10. Behave Ethically and Profits Will Follow.

Understanding these profit principles and applying them to your business can increase the probability of your long-term success and improve your returns along the way.

## Profit Principle #1: Build a Business Based on Your Distinctive Competence

Distinctive competence is a combination of knowledge, experience, reputation, and achievement. If you can identify a need for a product or service in an industry where you have distinctive competence, you can substantially increase your probability of startup success. You can minimize the risks by utilizing your understanding of existing business models, customer relationships, market needs, gaps in product design, fulfillment challenges, pricing sensitivity, and competition. (Distinctive competence is explained in greater detail in chapter 2.)

Think through the following questions to identify your distinctive competence and its application to your business idea.

- Do you have a unique skill, special knowledge, experience, or talent?

- Does your skill or knowledge have value in the marketplace?

- Can you use your competence to create something unique, disruptive, or innovative?

- Can you use your distinctive competence to secure preorders?

- What additional competencies do you need to succeed?

- How can you fill the competency void?

After wrestling with these questions, and reflecting on my past success, I realized my distinctive competence was my intimate knowledge of the value drivers behind real estate outsourcing. Given my early success with outsourcing, I was certain that the commercial potential to bring this model to market was phenomenal. Every corporation or institution with 100 or more locations was a candidate for outsourcing. The value proposition for the customer was undeniable, and the profit potential for my new business was huge.

Your distinctive competence should be the source of your new business idea. It is the one thing that will set you apart from your competitors. Selecting and building a business around your distinctive competence is the first step toward profitability.

## Profit Principle #2: Develop and Deliver a Superior Value Proposition

A superior value proposition captures the essence of your product's unique benefits and how it solves a vexing customer problem, meets a critical need, or relieves severe pain better than anything else in the marketplace. The most efficient path to profit is a value proposition that clearly delineates what your customer will get and how they will get it. Through experience, I have learned that a value proposition with a crystal-clear quantification of benefits is easiest to sell and the most compelling to buy. (The value proposition is so important that I discuss it in greater detail in chapters 3 and 4 and delve into its application to sales in chapter 8. *The Startup Roadmap,* in appendix A, covers this topic as well.)

Consider the answers to these questions in formulating your value proposition.

- What is your product, and who is your customer?

- How does your product alleviate your customer's pain?

- What is the value of pain relief, or how will your customer benefit?

- Is your customer motivated to buy your product repeatedly to prevent pain?

- Does your product serve a large and growing market?

- Do you have a sustainable competitive advantage—a unique solution to pain?

A good way to test the strength of your value proposition is to reflect on your rationale for starting your business in the first place.

- When you decided to start your business, you developed a vision for delivering unique and differentiated value to your customers. What is the vision for your business?

- You planned to create value so substantial that your customers would be motivated to seek you out to buy your product over and over again. What unique value do you bring to your customers?

- Your product would serve a large and growing market, offering your customers unique benefits not available from competitors. What is your competitive advantage?

- Your product would be priced in proportion to the value created for your customer and produce substantial profits for your stakeholders. How does your customer measure value? How will you price your product? What is your price/value ratio?

USI's value proposition revolutionized the way corporations managed and controlled their real estate. Corporations were suffering from high overhead costs, which were dragging down their bottom lines. USI's solution resolved their pain by reducing real estate costs across the enterprise, saving them millions of dollars. We structured our outsourcing contracts as multiyear exclusives. By alleviating a major source of pain, USI enjoyed a 95 percent contract renewal rate while maintaining a 20 percent net profit margin.

## Profit Principle #3: Don't Start Up Until . . .

It is only natural that you struggle with the desire to start up while knowing that you do not have all the answers. At the same time, you realize that you will never start up if you attempt to answer every question. Recognizing this challenge, I developed a short list of questions entitled, Don't Start Up Until . . .

These questions center around your business model, but it only requires the back of an envelope for you to figure out how you are going to make money; how much it is going to cost to run your business; and how soon you will reach breakeven and generate a profit.

Your ability to secure preorders will not only validate your business model, but will have a direct impact on your funding requirements, which will influence ownership and control.

Remember, you only need rough estimates to validate your business model, but you will need firm preorders to launch. Tackling the following six business model imperatives will give you confidence that you are ready to start up.

1. Don't start up until you know how you're going to generate revenue (simple estimates will suffice).
    a. How many customers are there?
    b. How much product will each customer buy?
    c. How will you price your product (share of value, cost-plus, market pricing)?
    d. Calculate revenue by estimating monthly sales (customers × units × price).
    e. Calculate revenue per quarter and revenue per year.

2. Don't start up until you understand how much it will cost to run your business (do your homework on expenses).
    a. How much will it cost to produce your product (manufacturing & distribution)?
    b. Who will be on your management team, and how much will it cost to compensate them (equity and/or salary)?
    c. How many employees will you need to start up, and what will it cost to compensate them (salary & medical)?

d. Where will you work, and how much will it cost (rent & utilities per month/year, furniture costs, supplies, etc.)?

e. How will you communicate with your customers and how much will it cost (computers, printers, mobile phones, Internet access, hosting, cloud services, etc.)?

f. How will you brand the business (logo, website, blog, social media, business cards, letterhead, signage, etc.)?

g. How much will it cost to sell your product (marketing, travel, entertainment, proposal generation, ongoing pursuit costs, etc.)?

h. How much will it cost for risk management and compliance (legal, accounting, & insurance)?

3. Don't start up until you know how you're going to make a profit (back of the envelope).

a. Revenues *minus* costs *equals* profit or (loss).

4. Don't start up until you have preorders to validate your business model and liftoff plans.

5. Don't start up until you have lined up the funding you need to reach breakeven (typically 18 months of operating capital).

a. Estimate how long it will take you to reach breakeven.

b. Determine your startup and operating capital needs.

c. Generate a list of funding sources and alternatives.

d. Secure the necessary funding with a cushion for unanticipated challenges (sensitive to imperative #6 below).

6. Don't start up until you have a crystal-clear understanding of the impact of your choice of startup funding on cost and control.

   a. Self-funding or bootstrapping will maximize control and avoid outside partners and interest payments.

   b. Selling equity will avoid interest payments but reduce control by introducing outside partners.

   c. Raising debt financing will let you maintain control by avoiding outside partners but will require interest payments.

I completed the financial modeling portion of this exercise in my kitchen with my two founding partners. We hashed things out with a flip chart and markers until we were comfortable that we had a financial model that would work. It took about two months to figure things out and be confident that we were on the right track. I completed the preorder portion of this exercise by meeting in the field with my first two customers: Patterson Dental and IDS Financial Services (now known as Ameriprise). Once we had these orders in hand, along with our financial model, we were able to make the decision to bootstrap and launch.

## Profit Principle #4: Take Charge of the Money and Control It

Your decision to build a profitable business is directly proportional to your ability to take charge of the money. Taking control of your money is a commitment to take responsibility for all of the following financial disciplines:

- Developing a realistic budget and operating the business within it

- Understanding how the timing of revenues and expenses affects cash flow

- Keeping a stranglehold on salaries and operating expenses

- Retaining your earnings for reinvestment as a first priority

Develop the discipline to generate and review simple financial reports and budgets on a daily basis until you achieve breakeven. Thereafter, continue with this financial discipline on a weekly basis until you achieve consistent profitability and hire a qualified financial officer that you can trust. Besides sleeping better at night, you will gain a clear understanding of the rhythm and flow of your revenues and expenses and their impact on your operating budget.

During USI's first three years of operation, I knew where every dollar of revenue came from and where every dollar was spent. I reviewed makeshift financial reports every single night and made judgments about budgets every day. We started out with a one-write checkbook system, quickly shifted to Excel to generate budgets and financial reports, and later migrated to QuickBooks as our primary financial management system. Throughout the life of USI, I always stayed very close to the money, and I was very cautious about extending trust when it came to the money. As a result, I was never surprised and slept peacefully most nights.

## Profit Principle #5: Create a Profit-Based Reward Structure

A profit-based reward structure compensates your management team for achievement of financial goals and your sales force for developing profitable new business. Rewarding performance with a percentage of profits is a surefire way to turn your management team and your sales force into P&L managers. Think about it. If your management team and your sales force can only increase their personal income when the business is generating a profit, then the business is almost guaranteed to make a profit.

At USI, we compensated our management team and our sales force with a moderate base salary to cover living expenses. At the same time, USI offered unlimited upside potential based on the generation of genuine profits. This type of reward structure aligned the financial interests of the producer with the financial interests of the business. Of course, we established profitability guidelines to ensure we achieved the desired financial results.

This incentive system required the management team and the sales force to become intimate with the financial model behind the business. Said another way, if your upside is tied to the generation of profit, you have to understand how much profit is generated by each dollar of revenue after costs. At USI, we pushed the responsibility for profit and loss management all the way down the organization.

As much as possible, we maximized the contribution and accountability of every professional by connecting them to an income-producing role. This operating model minimized USI's overhead by keeping a lid on non-income-producing staff.

## Profit Principle #6: Recognize and Hire "Lightning in a Bottle"

As you are scaling your business, you will be faced with the challenge to stretch beyond your comfort zone and reach to hire special talent. While I believe in developing and promoting internal management, sometimes you need to make the big external hiring decision to enable the business to realize its full potential.

As the business leader, you need to step up and make these transformational personnel decisions. It's not always comfortable or convenient, but sometimes you really can catch lightning in a bottle. This kind of talent only comes along once in a while. When it does, it can unlock business value and catalyze strategic growth. Even though this type of hiring decision may involve an aggressive compensation package, including a share of equity and control, it can be well worth the price to achieve your strategic vision.

Recognizing strategic leadership and acting decisively to bring it on board can revolutionize your business model, transform your organizational structure, and engineer the strategy to scale the business. It certainly did for me. I had the opportunity to make four critical hiring decisions that changed the trajectory of USI:

1. Rick Bertasi became President and Chief Operating Officer. Rick reengineered USI's business model, upgraded the organizational structure, implemented our annual business planning process, developed our customer-facing technology, and catalyzed our growth plans.

2. Nick Westley became USI's West Region President & Chief Strategy Officer. Nick opened up the western half of the US market, laid the foundation for our geographic profit centers, sculpted and quantified USI's value proposition, and developed our strategic growth plan.

3. Michael Casolo became USI's President of Design & Construction. Michael conceived the Space and Projects business, laid the foundation for our Line-of-Business profit centers, developed the Design & Construction business model, and hired a geographically distributed staff of architects and project managers.

4. Kip Chaffee became USI's Chief Financial Officer. Kip re-designed USI's internal operating model, re-engineered our financial & accounting system, developed USI's technology development team, and played a crucial role in facilitating our sale to Johnson Controls.

I was very fortunate. I had captured lightning in a bottle four times. These talented leaders played a vital role in USI's growth and the ultimate value realized when we sold the business. Recognizing the opportunity to reach and hire strategic leadership will enable you to scale your business and realize its full potential.

## Profit Principle #7: Create Profit Centers to Scale Your Business

Determining how you will scale your business will be one of your biggest challenges. After assessing numerous growth strategies, we came to realize that expansion based on the *profit motive* could be the key to our continued success. If we established geographic and line-of-business profit centers, we could drive growth by distributing profit and loss responsibility across the organization.

As a result, we embarked on a strategy to develop and deploy profit centers throughout USI. Each new P&L manager had the responsibility to generate new revenue, control expenses, and enhance profit performance. We scaled the business by creating four different kinds of profit centers:

- Regional P&Ls to expand geographic coverage
- Line-of-business P&Ls to build product lines

- Account-based P&Ls to grow existing customer relationships
- New business P&Ls to create new customer relationships

There are five steps to consider in formulating your plan to scale around profit centers.

1. Think through your current and potential customers' product and service requirements.

2. Assess your product and service fulfillment plans.

3. Formulate your new business development and sales plans.

4. Determine your geographic and line-of-business coverage plans.

5. Recruit, hire, and train qualified P&L managers for each profit center.

Based on our customers' requirements, USI created a combination of regional profit centers and line-of-business profit centers. Our regional profit centers enabled us to stay close to our customers, expand geographic coverage, and distribute financial responsibility. Our line-of-business profit centers focused managers on product-line performance, improved service delivery, and enhanced new product development. We also created account-based P&Ls for every account and new business P&Ls within each regional P&L.

Although complex, this profit-oriented growth model helped us achieve our financial objectives as we scaled the business.

## Profit Principle #8: Augment Profits with Proprietary Applications

Application software tools can generate new revenues and form the basis for a stand-alone profit center. Besides streamlining work processes and improving service delivery, software applications can enable your customers to manage workflows, eliminate process steps, and gain access to critical information. Proprietary applications can be so powerful that they can form a mutually dependent relationship between you and your customer.

Here are some of the questions you should consider when devising your strategy for developing proprietary application software:

- What information do your customers need to make better decisions?

- What tools do your customers need to better manage their work?

- How can you help your customers eliminate process steps and reduce operating costs?

- Are there software applications available in the market that solve these problems?

- If the applications are not available, can you develop proprietary applications to solve these problems?

- How can you utilize homegrown applications to tighten the link with your customers?

- Will your software applications create a sustainable competitive advantage?

- Can these applications create new revenue lines?

- Can these new revenue lines be used to form a stand-alone profit center?

As USI customers expanded around the world, they needed a reliable real estate management system to keep track of critical dates, projects, workflows, and costs. Initially, we devised a plan to develop a low-cost proprietary software application. However, since the dotcom boom was in full swing, we decided to take a step back to look at available market alternatives—there were over 300 new real estate applications coming online. We engaged a major consulting firm to cull the list and study "buy, build, or partner" scenarios. To our dismay, the consultant's final recommendation was a very costly custom-built solution.

Recognizing the limits of our customers' budgets, we came back full circle to developing a low-cost, proprietary software application that would serve 80 percent of the need at 20 percent of the cost. Our goal was to meet most of our customers' needs at a budget they all could afford. We called our application Sequentra. It was named after our customers' primary need to "sequentially track" project work and expenses around the globe. Based on Sequentra's revenue potential, we organized the application as a stand-alone profit center. Sequentra integrated all of our service lines into a single reporting dashboard for all of our customers.

Sequentra tightened the link with our customer base and created a barrier to entry for our competitors. It grew to become one of the dominant corporate real estate software solutions in the industry.

## Profit Principle #9: Build a Financial War Chest for Strategic Advantage

Once your business starts to generate consistent profits, you should retain your earnings to strengthen your balance sheet for strategic advantage. Naturally, there will be temptations to spend by increasing salaries, changing travel and expense limits, enhancing benefits, hiring unnecessary staff, or upgrading offices. If you can increase revenues while holding the line on expenses, you can begin to build a financial war chest.

At USI, we chose to stockpile our earnings. At first, we were just concerned about staying in business and having funds available for a rainy day. Then, as we continued to build our war chest, we gained confidence that we could make expansion decisions without the need for a bank or outside funding. It was interesting to discover that the less we needed the banks, the more they wanted to lend us their money. The same was true with private equity firms; they loved our growth trajectory, income statement, and balance sheet. They couldn't believe that we had no debt and that we had accumulated retained earnings of almost 20 percent of annual sales. As a result, the leverage shifted in favor of USI in all of our financial negotiations.

We built a balance sheet so formidable that we were able to offer $1 million advances on projected savings to win multiyear corporate outsourcing contracts (see "The Hail Mary" in chapter 8). This offer became a strategic weapon so powerful that it increased our close rate to over 50 percent.

Like most sacrifices, employing financial disciplines early and building a financial war chest can shift the balance of power and pay substantial dividends in the future. Imagine what you can achieve if you have such significant cash reserves that you are not reliant on third-party sources to grow your business.


## A Few Words about Spending

Of course, we did increase spending as the business grew, but we were always spending much less than the amount of money we were making. Since we paid our producers (executives, management, sales, account leaders, and delivery professionals) a moderate base salary with an *unlimited upside* based on profits, we were not under pressure to increase salaries. We maintained very strict travel and entertainment standards throughout the life of the business. For example, we capped airfares and used flight miles if the trip cost exceeded the cap. For the most part, we shared hotel rooms and lived within a moderate per diem for food.

In regard to benefits, we provided medical coverage from the beginning. Beyond that, I had made an early decision not to add other benefits until I knew I would never have to take them away. USI's benefits program grew to include dental, vision, sick days, personal days, maternity leave, extended vacation, short-term disability, long-term disability, term life insurance, 50 percent match on 401(k), etc. We never reduced or eliminated a benefit, so we never had to deal with morale issues around the loss of benefits.

Over time, we upgraded our offices and expanded staff carefully. Since every producer was paid on profit, expense bloating was never an issue. Finally, we never implemented a company car-, boat-, or aircraft-leasing program. I knew that we had done something right when Johnson Controls remarked that USI had the cleanest set of financials of any acquisition that they had ever made. Their sentiments were reflected in the purchase price.

## Profit Principle #10: Behave Ethically and Profits Will Follow

From the outset, I was committed to building a culture of trust and integrity. I had learned the importance of business ethics from some of the finest corporations in the world, including IBM and Hewlett-Packard. These companies enjoyed tremendous profit and growth while going out of their way to teach, manage, and deliver principled behavior. It seemed very clear to me that you could do the right thing, feel very good about it, and make plenty of money. Profits did not come at the expense of ethical behavior. Quite the contrary—profits resulted from ethical behavior.

I have had the opportunity to work for some terrific managers who set the bar on ethical standards. Likewise, I have been burned by bosses who exercised poor judgment and acted with a lack of integrity. Some of these painful experiences left scars that will never go away. When starting USI, I made a pact with myself that I would build a business where integrity was nurtured and mismanagement would not be tolerated. I felt so strongly about the importance of ethical behavior and mutual accountability that every employment offer included the following language:

> This employment offer is based on your commitment to USI's Standard Business Practices and Operating Philosophy including the following:
>
> - Making commitments and keeping them
> - Providing total quality and integrity in everything you do
> - Being a team player
> - Holding yourself accountable to the USI team
> - Holding the USI team accountable to you

By documenting our commitment to a culture of integrity, we strengthened all our internal and external relationships.

Beyond offer letters, we made it clear to all employees that we understood that every now and then a mistake would inevitably happen. We wanted to create an environment where employees were not afraid to acknowledge mistakes. We knew that apologizing for a mistake right away would enhance trust, whereas attempting to cover up mistakes would only damage relationships. Our motto was to acknowledge mistakes early and, when appropriate, make reparations. Using this simple, straightforward approach of acknowledging mistakes saved us millions in legal fees and built powerful and profitable long-term customer relationships.

Ethical behavior influenced every aspect of our business. We believed in fulfilling every promise in every contract and paying every employee and vendor in full and on time. We wanted everyone to know how much we valued and appreciated their relationships. We knew ethical behavior engendered loyalty and trust.

## SUMMARY: THE TEN COMMANDMENTS OF STARTUP PROFIT

Having the discipline to apply these profit principles will increase your probability of long-term success.

1. Build a Business Based on Your Distinctive Competence

2. Develop and Deliver a Superior Value Proposition

3. Don't Start Up Until . . .

    a. You know how you're going to generate revenue.

    b. You know how much it will cost to run your business.

    c. You know how you're going to make a profit.

    d. You have preorders to validate your business model and liftoff plans.

    e. You have lined up the funding you need to reach breakeven.

    f. You understand the impact of startup funding on cost and control.

4. Take Charge of the Money and Control It

5. Create a Profit-Based Reward Structure

6. Recognize and Hire "Lightning in a Bottle"

7. Create Profit Centers to Scale Your Business

8. Augment Profits with Proprietary Applications

9. Build a Financial War Chest for Strategic Advantage

10. Behave Ethically and Profits Will Follow

*Tom, Ed, and Gus with the Entrepreneur of the Year Award.*

## TRANSITIONING FROM GROWTH TO EXIT

Implementing these profit principles had a dramatic effect on USI's growth and profitability. In 2001, USI was acknowledged as one of the fastest growing companies and included in the Inc. 500. That same year, I was honored as Entrepreneur of the Year by Ernst & Young in the outsourcing category. It seemed that all the pieces were in place for continued growth and achievement.

As you'll read in the next chapter, we pursued an international expansion strategy that included both a major acquisition and an outright sale. To stay ahead of the competition, we needed to globalize the business and expand our suite of services.

SECTION

4

—

EXIT

# 10

## REALIZING VALUE

As the majority owner of USI, I had never contemplated a sale of the company. We were executing our strategic plan, which was based on consistent organic growth, with steady increases in revenues and profits. Having bootstrapped USI from the beginning without relying on outside funding, we had established a discipline early on to build a war chest of retained earnings to fund our growth and expansion. Since USI management was paid handsomely out of profits and we had no pressure from external investors, we had little motivation to increase business risk through an acquisition or to seek a liquidity event.

From my perspective, the beauty of bootstrapping your business is that you and your partners will be able to decide how and when to realize value. Somewhere in the back of my mind, I always thought that I'd pass the business down to my children. But that was far in the future, so I was glad that I didn't have impatient investors breathing down my neck, looking to get their money out.

## PRIVATE EQUITY

As USI hit its rapid growth stage and garnered industry recognition, we were often approached by private equity firms that wanted to invest in USI. It was ironic that we were being offered growth capital at the time when we least needed it.

The private equity (PE) conversations typically went something like this:

> USI: "Why would we want to sell our equity now?"
>
> PE: "You could use our money to fund exponential growth."
>
> USI: "We are already funding a 40 percent annual growth rate out of free cash flow."
>
> PE: "Well, you could take money out of the business for yourselves."
>
> USI: "We are comfortable with our profit-sharing arrangements and our growing equity value."

The USI executive team just couldn't see a reason why we should sell a piece of the company to a private equity firm. We had plenty of cash on hand to fund our growth, and we didn't need any money to make an acquisition.

A few years later, however, we heard about a huge opportunity that would require substantial outside funding. We realized at that point that private equity could play an important role in filling this need.

# QUANTUM GROWTH OPPORTUNITY

The story played out as follows. Early in 2001, we learned that Grubb & Ellis (GBE), the third largest real estate firm in the United States at the time, was for sale. Grubb & Ellis was listed on the NYSE and had over $400 million in annual revenue. Pursuing Grubb & Ellis as an acquisition could transform USI from an outsourcing-only business to a full-service, global real estate provider.

We knew that GBE had a large facilities management business that could meld nicely with USI's real estate outsourcing business. Additionally, GBE had the largest commercial real estate brokerage network in the nation, as well as a partnership with a large international real estate advisor named Knight Frank. Finally, GBE had a capital markets and appraisal business that could enhance USI's overall service offering.

The more we thought about the potential acquisition, the more excited we became. USI could become one of the largest contract service providers with almost $500 million in annual revenues, serving the Americas, Europe, and Asia. Overnight, our aspirations changed from being a US provider dependent on organic growth to becoming a global end-to-end service provider. In order to move the ball forward, we needed to line up an investment banker.

## Finding an Investment Banker (IB)

USI's chief strategy officer, Nick Westley, suggested that we meet with his close friend, Mike Rosenberg, an investment banker based in Los Angeles. Nick and Mike had become friends at Harvard Business School. Normally, I would have wanted to work with an investment banker closer to USI's headquarters in Connecticut, but I trusted Nick so much that I agreed to meet with Mike.

After getting to know Mike and his team at Barrington Associates, I felt completely at ease about working with them. Before we got started, we negotiated the contract to have Barrington represent us in pursuit of Grubb & Ellis. At first I was surprised at the size of their fee, which was based on a percentage of the purchase price, but I soon realized that we could not get the job done without a high-quality and trustworthy investment bank. (Barrington Associates was sold to Wells Fargo in 2006, and the successor firm is known as Intrepid Investment Bankers.)

Here is how USI went about selecting our investment banker. You may find these criteria useful when selecting your investment banker.

### Selecting an Investment Banker

1. Secure a qualified referral from a person you trust.

2. Qualify the banker's experience based on—
    a. Years of investment banking experience
    b. Number and value of completed deals
    c. Comparable transactions in your industry
    d. List of references with contact information

3. Understand the banker's methodology regarding their—
    a. Process for buying a company
    b. Process for selling a company

4. Assess satisfaction level of other banking clients.

5. Quantify the IB firm's support team and connections.

6. Ensure there is a good fit with IB firm's contact point.

7. Understand the IB firm's contract terms and fees.

8. Make sure there is strong level of trust with the IB firm.

## GBE Due Diligence

Once we organized our pursuit strategy and due-diligence teams, we flew to Chicago to conduct management interviews at Grubb & Ellis's headquarters. Since GBE was a public company, there was a great deal of information available. After interviewing GBE senior leadership, we delved into the firm's financials.

The Barrington team participated extensively in the due diligence; produced the consolidated pro forma; introduced numerous private equity partners that could provide capital; organized how we would raise the necessary debt financing; and structured a deal in which USI would maintain a controlling interest. USI and the selected private equity firm agreed to a 60/40 ownership split for the proposed new entity. We intended to take GBE private. This would allow us to get our arms around the business without the pressure and expense a public company faces with quarterly reporting and SEC filing requirements.

## Selecting a Private Equity (PE) Firm

Selecting a private equity firm calls for extensive due diligence to ensure you will be working with people whom you can trust. Besides providing capital, selecting the right private equity firm can open the door to new strategic partners, specialized industry experience, access to new customers, and support in recruiting key executives. On the other hand, selecting the wrong partner can be very painful, disabling, and quite possibly destructive. We took the following steps when selecting our private equity partner:

### Private Equity Selection Criteria

1. Secure a qualified referral from a person you trust.

2. Qualify the PE firm based on available investment capital.

3. Assess satisfaction level of other investment recipients.

4. Quantify the PE firm's capabilities and connections.

5. Understand the PE firm's investment time frame for exit.

6. Ensure there is a good fit with the PE firm's contact point.

7. Negotiate the PE firm's transaction and management fees.


## The Consolidation Plan

Our plan was to create a holding company with two major subsidiaries: USI's contract business and Grubb & Ellis's transactions business. All of Grubb & Ellis's facilities management and contract work would become part of USI's outsourcing business, and USI's transactions business would become part of Grubb & Ellis's brokerage business.

Combining our companies made sense strategically and financially. Both companies had very strong free cash flow, and neither company had any debt, so taking on debt to make the purchase was eminently doable. Only one step remained.


## Conflicting Interests

It turned out that the largest shareholder of Grubb & Ellis's stock was Warburg Pincus, a global private equity firm. After meeting with Warburg's lead partner on the deal, we agreed to send our letter of intent to GBE management to purchase all of their outstanding stock. The Warburg partner agreed to review our offer with GBE's board and make a decision.

A few weeks later, GBE's board of directors informed us that they had decided to recapitalize the company with debt financing instead of selling the company. Our deal was off. We believed that USI's letter of intent helped establish a value for Grubb. We surmised that GBE utilized our valuation to justify a new capital structure, which included taking on substantial debt and paying out a hefty dividend. Naturally, we were disappointed that the deal came apart.

Ironically, soon thereafter, Warburg sold its interest in GBE, and the company subsequently struggled under the weight of the debt that it had taken on. Its stock price dropped, and the firm was ultimately delisted from the NYSE. In 2012, Grubb filed for bankruptcy and was later sold.

Even though the acquisition never came to fruition, we accomplished a number of important objectives.

- We developed a deep trust relationship with Mike Rosenberg and Barrington Associates, which would become very useful to USI in the years ahead.

- We established the parameters and methodology for a market valuation for USI for the first time.

- We learned how to value an acquisition, structure a complex deal, line up a private equity partner, and organize significant bank debt.

## REFOCUS ON GROWTH

After the Grubb & Ellis deal fell apart, we refocused on growing USI organically. It was easy to get back on track because USI's new business engine was firing on all cylinders. Our revenues continued growing at a 40 percent compounded annual rate, while our profits climbed. We kept adding new accounts, while growing existing accounts as the GBE deal faded into the past.

Since we had completed our first formal business valuation, the topic of business sale and recapitalization started to come up more frequently at partner meetings. But I had no interest in selling, unless the strategic growth opportunity was so significant that it was worth getting external investors involved. We had a very talented leadership team, and we continued to build strong brand equity in the marketplace. And naturally, I liked having control over the business.

## COMPETITIVE DIFFERENTIATION

Even though we were in competition with much larger firms like Jones Lang LaSalle and CBRE, USI was flourishing. We succeeded through speed, creativity, and superior service execution—winning more than our fair share of Fortune 500 accounts.

USI had negotiated outsourcing contracts with some of the best brands in American industry including Boeing, Computer Sciences Corporation, General Electric, T-Mobile, and United Technologies. Our strategic focus, process expertise, open-book cost model, and customized value proposition made a huge difference in attracting and keeping high-profile clients.

Based on customer satisfaction, USI was able to maintain a 95 percent contract renewal rate. Customer loyalty and growth came from the simple fact that we saved our customers millions in occupancy costs. To help our customers gain control of their real estate, we analyzed their portfolios to get answers to the following questions:

- What real estate did they have?
- How much real estate did they need?
- How could they optimize their real estate?
- What could we do to reduce their real estate costs?
- How much could we help them save?
- How would we measure savings?
- How would we organize to get the work done?

The process of answering these questions proved to be highly effective in unlocking potential savings for our customers. For example, Computer Sciences Corporation (CSC) reduced its real estate costs by $35 million in our first year working together. CSC's chief financial officer, Lee Level, was so pleased with our results that he agreed to provide a testimonial ad for USI in *CFO* magazine as shown below.

*Lee Level testimonial ad in* CFO *magazine*

As discussed in chapter 8, "Sales is a Contact Sport," testimonials and referrals were USI's most effective business development tool.

## TROUBLE AHEAD

We continued to enjoy solid growth in the early years of the new millennium, but trouble was looming on the horizon.

More and more customers wanted USI to expand into facilities management (FM)—the coordination of space, people, and infrastructure. As a stopgap measure, we partnered with FM service providers to address this need. Beyond facilities management, our multinational customers were concerned about global coverage. Even though we did our best to sell around this issue, we expected that the day of reckoning was coming.

### Breaking Point

In early 2004, two of our most prominent clients, Computer Science Corporation and T-Mobile, each made it clear to us that they wanted a single point of contact for real estate services that included facilities management. Our partnering approach with FM providers would no longer suffice.

Additionally, CSC and T-Mobile were concerned about USI's lack of a global footprint. Even though we had some offices overseas and executed work in other countries, we did not have the scale and coverage CSC wanted. We needed to offer a global end-to-end solution or risk losing CSC and T-Mobile.

It gave me a sick feeling in the pit of my stomach to think that we could lose some of our biggest brands. If we did not solve this problem, we could be relegated to the position of a boutique real estate services provider. Something had to change.

# JOHNSON CONTROLS (JCI)

It just so happened that both CSC and T-Mobile contracted with Johnson Controls to handle their facilities management needs. JCI was a $25 billion provider of automotive systems and building controls that included a significant facilities management business.

Seemingly out of the blue, an executive from Johnson Controls called me to open a dialogue about a potential merger. It turned out that Lee Level had encouraged JCI to contact us. Lee realized that we needed one another. Johnson Controls had the global platform and the facilities management business, while USI had the high-margin real estate services business. The idea of a merger with a company that complimented our offerings started to intrigue us. Soon enough, Johnson Controls asked USI senior partners to travel to its headquarters in Milwaukee for a strategic business review to assess the concept of a combination.

## The Secret Sauce

Shortly thereafter, we met at JCI headquarters. We discussed the business opportunity and strategic fit. Johnson Controls admired our ability to attract new customers, establish long-term relationships, and then grow accounts by selling additional products and services. Based on our joint review, it seemed clear that we could help one another expand service lines and cross-sell into each other's accounts.

"The reason we are interested in USI is for the secret sauce," said one JCI executive. He explained that secret sauce was a unique mixture of creativity, innovation, skill, speed, and tenacity. To him (and to us), it represented the magic formula that made an entrepreneurial company like USI so special.

Inevitably, as mature companies evolve, they lose the flexibility to innovate by adding layers of management that rely on legacy systems to control risk. In the process, they have a hard time holding onto their own secret sauce. They have an even harder time trying to create it. In our case, Johnson Controls was looking to buy it.

Our meeting ended with a request from JCI's senior management to grant them an exclusive to negotiate the purchase of all of USI's stock. I responded that we were interested but that I would need to review it with my partners and my investment banker.

## THE USI AUCTION

In September 2004, we contacted Mike Rosenberg at Barrington Associates for advice. As we talked with Mike, it became clear that USI had reached a peak performance window, making the timing right for a sale. Although I had been adamant about maintaining control of USI, I knew the outsourcing market was changing, the competition was closing in, and we needed to take action.

Given our challenges with CSC and T-Mobile, I became an advocate for the sale to Johnson Controls. The combination had the potential to create a powerhouse without any personnel reduction or service redundancy. The JCI–USI merger would instantly make the combination the biggest player in the global real estate outsourcing industry. We would be in position to fulfill our customers' needs for a global end-to-end solution while asserting the financial strength of a $25 billion international company.

In December 2004, after much discussion with USI senior partners, I called Mike and told him that we were ready to sell the company. Although USI partners would no longer be owners, we could monetize our equity at peak value.

As I thought about the decision, it dawned on me that our small startup, which I had bootstrapped, had grown into a very valuable company. After the acquisition, we would be able to offer even more to our customers as part of a worldwide corporation. The entire firm would be vaulted into a new, more powerful position. I was excited.

I told Mike that I really liked the combination of USI and JCI. "The demands for USI's services could go through the roof," I said. "That would eliminate any concern about potential staff reductions." I suggested we concede to JCI's request for an exclusive.

Mike said, "There is no way you should offer JCI an exclusive. We need to run an auction to maximize the purchase price for the company. This will also ensure that JCI makes a competitive bid."

Then he added, "It is my job to get the best price for you and your partners. Follow my direction and we will get the deal done with the best buyer." Mike relayed that "while we are producing the offering memorandum, JCI can have a virtual exclusive" prior to presenting the company to other potential bidders. In effect, JCI's leaders had the chance to make an early bid for USI six weeks before the market at large became aware of the opportunity.

Mike suggested that I reconnect with JCI executives to let them know that we would be producing a formal offering memorandum and running an auction to sell the company. After I contacted JCI executives, they stated that they would like to formulate their offer in advance of the auction. They also asked when we would be completing the offering memorandum, as they needed time to put their bid together and secure the CEO's approval to submit it.

## OFFERING MEMORANDUM

An offering memorandum is a bound booklet that presents salient facts and figures about a company that is for sale. It is sent to

potential purchasers when they express an interest in acquiring a
company and have signed a confidentiality agreement.

The offering memorandum presents a compelling argument by
discussing the business, its achievements, and its future growth
potential, including disclaimers and risks. A comprehensive offering
memorandum includes all of the following elements:

- Executive summary
- History and background
- Services
- Client relationships
- Sales and marketing
- Facilities and operations
- Management, employees, and ownership
- Financial performance
- Industry and competition
- Exhibits

The offering memorandum is prepared by an investment banker
working in combination with the majority owners. Typically, the
investment bankers are paid a retainer for front-end expenses as an
advance against their share of the sales price. Success fees on middle-
market transactions range from five percent on smaller deals to as
little as three quarters of one percent on larger deals.

Barrington played a key role in working with USI to develop the
offering memorandum. In order to assemble the volume of information needed, we divided our team into three work groups.

- Group 1 was tasked with assembling customer and sales projections, corporate history, and marketing materials.

- Group 2 was focused on producing financial & accounting records and making financial projections.

- Group 3 was responsible for organizing legal, compliance, and risk documentation.


Group 1 gathered the customer and sales information that fed the financial projections. Rick Bertasi, Nick Westley, and I developed detailed spreadsheets demonstrating prior performance and projecting future performance including new contracts, renewals, and expansions over a five-year period. This provided potential buyers with current and future valuation information.

Group 2 had the biggest challenge. As a small, privately held company, USI worked with an accountant, Bill Turnof, who provided us with *reviewed* financial statements. We soon discovered that we were required to produce the more complex and expensive *audited* financial statements. Kip Chaffee, our CFO, had the responsibility to select an accounting firm to produce the audited financial statements for the prior three years and complete this work within a 45-day window. Kip and his team ultimately hired the accounting firm McGladrey to work in combination with Bill Turnof to produce the audited financials. Given the time frame, this was a very tall order.

Group 3 was headed by Dominick Modugno, USI's general counsel, working in combination with Ridg Barker from our law firm, Kelley Drye & Warren. Dominick coordinated with Ridg and his team to produce the details of our corporate structure, professional license information, compliance records, and a list of potential risks.

All of this information was assembled for two purposes: first, to provide potential buyers with important facts and figures about the business for the information memorandum and, second, to provide those potential buyers with critical validation data. This detailed information was made available in a data room at our headquarters during on-site management interviews.

## CREATING LEVERAGE

Mike and his team put together a list of more than 50 different potential bidders divided into three buckets: strategic buyers, private equity firms, and industry competitors. In most cases, a strategic buyer will pay the highest price because the acquired asset has the potential to unlock and enhance total enterprise value. We were excited because we knew that Johnson Controls was a strategic buyer.

Soon enough, the offering memorandum was complete. We were ready to start the auction process and find out what USI was really worth. Before getting the auction underway, I had agreed to reconnect with my executive contact at Johnson Controls. I had high hopes that JCI had used the virtual exclusive period to formulate an offer for USI.

I called my contact point at JCI the night before the offering memorandum was scheduled to be distributed. Much to my surprise and disappointment, my contact said JCI executive management was not ready to make an offer. He reconfirmed his determined interest in purchasing USI, asking us to delay the auction and extend the exclusive period. I bit down hard, swallowed deep, and said that we were committed to sticking with our plan to distribute the offering memorandum in the morning. I was very frustrated at this turn of events but followed Mike's advice to maintain the integrity of the schedule and continue with the auction.

Even though we were gambling that JCI might walk away from the acquisition, we knew we were doing the right thing to stand firm. As Mike had explained, we needed to keep control of our destiny. By having a public auction, we could discover what USI was truly worth. Competition would help maximize our valuation.

## Optimizing Value

The next day, Barrington began the auction process by sending out a notification-of-sale letter with an executive summary to the 50 prospects on its list. As part of the process, we called JCI management and asked if they would like to receive the offering memorandum. They said, "Of course," but expressed frustration that we were moving ahead without them.

Within two weeks, Barrington received 14 formal responses from qualified buyers willing to sign the non-disclosure agreement and requesting a copy of the offering memorandum. About 10 days later, we received eight offers to purchase, specifying preliminary purchase prices and requesting dates for management interviews and access to the data room. The preliminary purchase offers were in the ballpark on the valuation of USI, but we did not yet have an offer from Johnson Controls.

Recognizing that we were headed down a track to sell USI, I called Mike Rosenberg and suggested that I contact Johnson Controls one more time to solicit their bid. I continued to believe that joining with JCI, as opposed to other industry competitors, would enable USI to avoid any duplication of services. This meant we would not have to let any personnel go as a result of the acquisition. This was very important to me. Knowing that we had eight other parties that had already made offers, Mike concurred that I should make a final call to my contact at JCI.

When I connected with JCI, my contact restated his interest but said that he still needed more time to discuss the deal with his chairman and CEO, John Barth. I saw this request as an opening and suggested that Rick and I meet with John Barth directly to explain USI and our value proposition. Much to my surprise, my contact liked the idea and agreed to coordinate the meeting with his chairman.

Just a few hours later, he called back and asked us to fly out to Milwaukee by the end of the week. When Rick and I entered the JCI boardroom, there were at least eight JCI executives around the table. John Barth and Steve Roell, JCI's chief financial officer, peppered us with questions about USI's business and its strategic fit with JCI.

Then JCI's CEO asked, "How do you feel about being in the front seat with us in the back seat?" He knew that customers' real estate budgets typically had priority over facility management budgets—and hence, USI would be in the driver's seat with customers, relative to JCI's facilities management business.

I answered, "We would feel very comfortable in the front seat. More importantly, how would you feel?" Barth responded with a warm smile, and the meeting ended with the agreement that they would get back to us shortly.

When Rick and I landed back in New York, we had a message waiting from my contact at JCI.

"You guys hit the ball out of the park," he said. "We are going ahead with the deal. We will call you tomorrow to discuss terms."

Within two weeks, we agreed to sell 100 percent of USI's stock to Johnson Controls for $80 million. When factoring in cash on the balance sheet, accounts receivable, and funds in USI Investment Partners, we distributed an additional $20 million to USI shareholders, representing a total value of over $100 million. We had achieved our goal, realizing peak value by selling to a strategic buyer. The entire process had taken six months. USI had been in business as a private company for 14 years.

After the sale was closed in June 2005, I became president and CEO of the combined Johnson Controls real estate and facilities management business for North America and South America. Rick became president and CEO of Johnson Controls' facilities management business in Europe, the Middle East, and Africa. Most of USI's senior management was promoted into leadership positions for the combined business throughout the Americas.

To optimize the secret sauce, after equity distributions, I set aside $2 million of the sale proceeds to use as continuity bonuses for our top people, encouraging them to stay on. My personal goal was to make this the best acquisition that Johnson Controls had ever made.

## THE VALUE OF FLEXIBILITY

Inevitably you will face challenges and opportunities that change preconceived notions about your business and its strategic direction. As the business leader, you need to be flexible and open to assess the potential to transform the business and unlock equity value.

While USI's strategic plan called for consistent organic growth, when the Grubb & Ellis situation presented itself, we needed to consider the possibility for radical change. Even though we did not complete the transaction, the pursuit of GBE had a dramatic impact on our strategic vision for the business. We developed aspirations to transform USI from a national provider to a global end-to-end provider.

Influenced by customer needs and competitive forces, we were ready to consider an outright sale rather than becoming a niche player. All of these factors opened our eyes to the potential for realizing value and the resources required to achieve that goal.

## Steps for Realizing Value

1. Make sure you have a strategic plan for your business.

2. Be flexible and open to new opportunities for change.

3. Stretch your thinking by assessing acquisitions and sales.

4. Develop selection criteria to qualify external advisors.

5. Ensure confidence, trust, and transparency in your advisors.

6. Clarify process, roles, and fee structure.

7. Organize due-diligence teams: bankers, lawyers, & accountants.

8. Leverage your bankers' experience and follow their advice.

9. Make sure to leverage competitive bids to optimize value.

10. Negotiate deal terms that are sensitive to long-term needs.

# 11

## PRESERVING THE SECRET SAUCE

In retrospect, I should have done a better job negotiating the post-sale operating terms and conditions for USI's sale to Johnson Controls. Yes, we were able to keep all of our employees without the need to relocate. But we were so caught up in the selling process and negotiating the purchase price that we took our eye off the ball on what life would be like after the sale.

At the risk of sounding ungrateful, I want to share what I learned and how things could have been done differently to produce a better result. In many respects, these lessons apply any time an entrepreneurial business is sold to a larger, more mature company.

Before discussing the integration challenges, I would be remiss not to highlight some of JCI's unique strengths and achievements. At the time of this writing, Johnson Controls is ranked number 66 on the Fortune 500 list and number 245 on the Fortune Global 500 list. JCI is routinely acknowledged as one of America's Most

Admired Companies by *Fortune* magazine, a Best Corporate Citizen by *Corporate Responsibility* magazine, and a member of the Billion Dollar Roundtable, spending more than $1 billion annually with diverse suppliers. I continue to be a shareholder with a strong belief in the long-term growth and aspirations of Johnson Controls.

## EARLY SIGNS OF DIVERGENCE

A couple of months after we sold USI to Johnson Controls, I remember being engaged in a particularly frustrating after-hours strategy phone call with my new JCI boss. We started to discuss business goals and the motivation systems to achieve them. The top-down corporate approach that I was hearing was in stark contrast to the entrepreneurial all-hands-on-deck mentality we had at USI. I became exasperated with the tone and direction of the call. I just didn't think my boss's approach was the best way to motivate the troops to accomplish the mission. Since I was still new to Johnson Controls, I held my tongue in an effort to integrate and conform to the JCI way.

As soon as I got off the phone, I started venting my concerns to my wife. My son overheard the discussion and said, "Relax, Dad, you got the Golden Fleece. The sale is complete, and the money is in the bank. Why are you getting so worked up?" On the surface, I could understand his point of view. After all, JCI did own the business and had control. But after years of leading my own company, I was programmed to make the decisions, set the strategy, and figure out how to get the job done. Frankly, I was used to having the control—after all, once an entrepreneur, always an entrepreneur.

Even though JCI claimed they were committed to *preserving the secret sauce*, I soon realized it was on their terms and under their direction. By selling USI, I had given up the reins. I needed to adjust and recognize that JCI was in control. This was difficult to digest. In retrospect, I could have softened the transition with a more thorough negotiation of the post-sale operating terms up front.

## THINK BEYOND THE SALE

Selling your business can create a substantial windfall, but it will come at the price of control. You need to think beyond the obvious strategic benefits and visualize the operating realities of your life after the sale. Your investment banker should optimize the sale price, but you need to take responsibility to negotiate the post-sale operating terms. Rather than assuming the buyer's commitment to preserve the secret sauce, you need to identify the ingredients that make your company great and negotiate their inclusion in the purchase and sale agreement. Based on continued performance and achievement, you also need to nail down your degree of autonomy and control after the sale. The following post-sale operating terms should be defined in the agreement:

- Preservation of vital ingredients in the secret sauce;
- Clarity on reporting structure and responsibility;
- Scope of decision-making authority;
- Definition of spending latitude and constraints;
- Control over recruiting and hiring;
- Influence on compensation and reward decisions;
- Input on integration time frame & budget; and
- Authority over business plan & implementation.

Even though we had influence over some of these control points, we could have done a better job hammering out the details. Negotiating the specific provisions in advance could have smoothed USI's integration into JCI and enhanced total value creation. Instead, we experienced a series of transitional challenges that diluted the full potential of the merger.

## HERE'S HOW IT HAPPENED

Immediately following the sale, everyone was excited about creating the world's largest global real estate and facilities management business. The combined revenues for the new global business unit exceeded $3 billion, while Johnson Controls' overall business revenues exceeded $25 billion. USI went from being one of the smallest real estate outsourcing players to the largest global outsourcing competitor in the field.

The executive responsible for the acquisition kept emphasizing the need for USI leadership to invigorate JCI's traditional facilities management business with the secret sauce. He defined USI's secret sauce as having five components:

1. The entrepreneurial spirit to innovate

2. The zeal to win every contest

3. A creative approach to problem solving

4. An aggressive culture and leadership

5. The drive to maximize value and profit

He repeatedly stressed his commitment to unleash the secret sauce as the means to revolutionize the business. This was empowering and music to our ears. In addition to merging USI's business with JCI's business in North America, he communicated a vision for acquiring more real estate companies in Europe and Asia. So much so that JCI executive management gave the green light to begin investigating alternatives for real estate service company acquisitions in Europe, with an eye toward Asia as well.

As the new leader of the Americas business, I had three key responsibilities: lead the integration, sort out the combined organizational structure, and develop the business plan. The first couple of months were a barrage of introduction and integration meetings. I needed to optimize the newly combined organization in the Americas without losing focus on the combined customer base.

It was a fast-paced and exciting time. Because JCI was in the facilities management business and USI was in the real estate services business, there were no redundant positions, and no one lost their job. Except for a few ruffled egos, JCI and USI were a perfect fit.

## CONSISTENT MANAGEMENT DISCIPLINES

Even though JCI was a hefty Fortune 100 company and USI was a midsize Inc. 500 company, we held a number of important management disciplines in common. Both companies utilized a comprehensive annual business planning process to project growth and measure performance against goals. We also conducted rigorous monthly business reviews to track progress, identify challenges, and minimize risk and surprises. Both cultures placed a heavy emphasis on encouraging teamwork, delegating responsibilities, and giving people the room to get things done. Both JCI and USI were committed to respect for the individual and doing the right thing. These shared values enhanced the integration and increased productivity.

The early stages of the JCI–USI integration went along quite smoothly until . . .

## THE YORK ACQUISITION

In early August 2005, just two months after we completed the merger, JCI announced its $3.2 billion acquisition of York International, a major player in the heating, ventilation, and air conditioning (HVAC) industry. This purchase transformed JCI overnight into one of the largest manufacturers, distributors, and service providers in the HVAC business. Looking back, I finally understood why John Barth, JCI's chairman and CEO at the time, had asked me how significant the United Technologies (UTC) contract was to USI. Barth had known that JCI's forthcoming acquisition of York International could create a serious upset for UTC's large air conditioning business unit, Carrier.

At first, it seemed as though things had just gotten even better for USI. We were awarded the internal contract to manage all of JCI's real estate, as well as all of York's real estate. The logic for the award was twofold:

1. The newly acquired USI team could meet the need to reduce operating costs by consolidating and eliminating redundant locations between JCI and York.

2. JCI needed to practice what it preached. How could JCI–USI sell the benefits of outsourcing to other corporations if Johnson Controls did not award their real estate management to their new acquisition, USI?

In effect, we had secured the contract for two Fortune 500 companies in one fell swoop. These were significant outsourcing contracts by any measure.

But the York acquisition led to one difficult transition after another.

## First Major Transition: Coaches Reassigned

Before the dust settled on the York acquisition, the lead JCI architects for the USI acquisition were reassigned; one to the HVAC service business in Europe and the other to a completely different business group. The newly merged global real estate and facilities management business was immediately tucked under the York acquisition. We were suddenly reporting into a York financial executive who had no prior knowledge of the real estate outsourcing business. It was comparable to being recruited by the coach of a run-and-shoot football offense and then transitioned to a coach committed to a three-yards-and-up-the-middle strategy. USI's leadership team was organized for fast-paced aggression, not a cautious, lumbering approach.

But I knew we needed to make the most of the change that was foisted upon us. I liked our new leader and figured that all we needed to do was make our numbers, and we would be left alone to run the business. I was wrong. Even though we consistently exceeded our financial goals, the lead executive scrutinized every decision. This restrained management style flew in the face of our run-and-shoot offense. We began to lose momentum, and I began to get frustrated. The term secret sauce was replaced with words like *follow the chain of command.*

Like most entrepreneurial companies, USI made decisions thoughtfully but quickly; we succeeded by trying new things, and we followed through with aggressive implementation. We competed on speed, innovation, and creativity. We were always in motion pursuing the next opportunity. This new, very cautious operating model was going to be a challenge.

## Second Major Transition: Integration and Cost-Reduction Goals

As soon as the York acquisition was announced, we were assigned aggressive integration and cost-reduction goals. The cost-reduction program was treated as a group-wide initiative to help justify the acquisition of York. Since the real estate and facilities management business had been achieving its numbers, and we were already lean, I felt an across the board cost-reduction program cut more muscle than fat. I knew that I needed to be a team player, but I was not happy making unnecessary staff reductions.

For example, the consolidation study recommended that we shut down USI's Manhattan sales office at the Seagram Building to consolidate into York's midtown service office. We were mixing dress coats and ties with hard hats and shirtsleeves. I saw this move as penny-wise and pound-foolish. We saved a few dollars, but we no longer had a viable meeting place for high-profile corporate clients. It seemed that little thought had been given to the space needs for high-level corporate sales versus the kind of space needed for an air conditioning service office. It was a huge step down in quality without conference rooms and private meeting space. I became so concerned about turnover that I called a special meeting with my New York management team. I wanted to make sure that we would not lose our top performers as a result of the consolidation. In the short term, we achieved our assigned integration and cost-reduction goals, but we paid a price later in lost sales and resignations.

## Third Major Transition: Assignment of Synergy and Pull-Through Sales Goals

Soon after the York acquisition, we were introduced to synergy goals and pull-through sales goals. Synergy goals were sales that could only be achieved by cross-selling USI services into JCI accounts and vice versa, whereas pull-through sales required our business unit to sell the products and services of the HVAC business units. The combination raised our business plan objectives from 20 percent year-over-year growth to about 35 percent—a very tall order.

As an entrepreneur, I like to stretch and achieve big things, but we were new to the JCI party. I did not want to be forced into over-promising and underdelivering. We were being asked to move the dial by 35 percent on a combined business that was 15 times larger than USI. I wanted to make sure that we overachieved to prove that we could be counted on. After all, proven performance breeds trust, which is usually rewarded with decision-making autonomy—a critical outcome to long-term success and happiness.

I was uncomfortable with a 35 percent growth goal, but I recognized that Johnson Controls was the new owner with the power to make that decision. I modified our business plan to conform and organized to meet the challenge. But then I learned that our top rainmaking talent was being relocated to Europe. I remember sitting down with my JCI boss to question the sanity of this decision. He agreed that the move made little sense given the size of the growth goals, but he was not empowered to change it. Slowly but surely, some of our most senior talent were distributed around the world. In one sense, it was a compliment to our leadership team. On the other hand, JCI was splintering USI into too many little pieces.

## Fourth Major Transition: The JCI Human Resources Machine

During our final due-diligence meeting just prior to the sale, we had met with John Barth, JCI chairman and CEO. He asked lots of questions, but the one question that stuck out most in my mind was when Barth asked, "If JCI purchases USI, how can we ensure that USI continues to generate a 20 percent profit?" My ability to make good on that goal soon faced a huge internal roadblock—JCI Human Resources (HR).

It seemed from day one, HR wanted to change USI's hiring practices, compensation methodology, and motivation systems. This confounded me. JCI had just purchased an entrepreneurial company in the real estate services space where they had no prior knowledge or experience. What did JCI know about hiring criteria and motivation systems in the real estate services industry? Why not listen and learn about what was needed and discover new ways to get things done? Over and over again, I emphasized that changing the reward structure would kill the goose that laid the golden eggs.

I found myself in a constant battle with Human Resources, while JCI executive management continued to verbally reinforce the need to *preserve the secret sauce*. I found myself between a rock and a hard place. I knew I could not back down because the most valuable ingredient in the secret sauce was our profit-based reward structure (see chapter 8's "Creating a Profit-Based Reward Structure" and chapter 9's Profit Principle #5). I was forced to spend more time on inside management than outside business development. Focusing on internal issues is the killer to business growth, productivity, and morale.

Here's why I fought so hard to keep our motivation system in place:

> With USI's motivation system, our producers (executives, P&L managers, account managers, and salespeople) were paid a base salary of about

$100,000 with a 10 percent profits interest in their defined area of responsibility. Producers had direct control over their financial rewards. Although salaries remained constant (a key factor in minimizing USI fixed overhead), the profit streams carried over from one year to the next. These profit streams kept building over time to produce a substantial annuity income stream (oftentimes exceeding $300,000 and sometimes exceeding $600,000). Growing this annuity kept pressure on each professional to maintain and grow existing accounts, to add new accounts each year, and to make sure each contract was consistently profitable. Naturally, everyone wanted to make more money each year, creating tremendous motivation to secure new accounts and expand existing accounts—hence USI's 40 percent compounded growth rate and consistent 20 percent net profit margin.

In contrast, JCI's system effectively doubled the base salary from $100,000 to $200,000 (this doubled fixed overhead), eliminated the profits interest, and provided an average 25 percent bonus (one half based on individual performance and one half based on business group performance). The financial outcome for a top performer averaged a $250,000 package.

On the surface, it seems pretty close: $250,000 plus stock vs. $300,000 with unlimited upside. However, there are three major flaws:

- First, doubling the base salary undercuts the motivation to overperform and doubles the fixed overhead on the business. If your base salary is $100,000 and you are fighting to make over $200,000 in profits interest, both the individual and the business do much better.

- Second, when you eliminate the profits interest, you eliminate the P&L mentality and the pressure to generate and control a profitable outcome. This stifles profit growth. Said another way, if you can make $200,000 without the pressure to produce, then why would you worry about maximizing profits—especially when new business prospects dried up during the Global Financial Crisis?

- Third, everyone likes to be in control of their destiny— especially when it comes to financial reward. An objective reward system is always better than a subjective reward system. If you raise the fixed salary and cap the upside, what is the motivation to overperform?

Suffice it to say, I knew that changing our motivation and reward structure would destroy the motivation to overperform—and I fought like hell to keep our entrepreneurial profit system in place.

## THE ROLE OF HUMAN RESOURCES

I believe that human resources is a staff function responsible to support the core business. Human resources should act as an enabler. Since line management is responsible for achieving profits and maintaining budgets, line management should stay in touch with all personnel decisions—particularly the producers. When human resources supports line management to enhance productivity, it can have a very positive effect on the business. However, when human resources is left unchecked and takes over the hiring decisions, it can have a very negative impact on financial performance, business growth, and—believe it or not—personnel.

In spite of JCI's human resources, I worked quite well with JCI line management and made my numbers 28 out of 30 months with a 42 percent year-over-year profit growth in my final year onboard. However, soon after I departed in December of 2007, human resources effectively doubled the base salaries and eliminated the profit-based reward structure—right before the Global Financial Crisis hit full stride.

## MAKING THE MARRIAGE WORK

As previously discussed, most entrepreneurial companies thrive on innovation, creativity, and speed as key ingredients for driving success. Entrepreneurs are willing to take risks to increase the probability of breakthrough achievement at the cost of possible failure. In many respects, these attributes get into the bloodstream of high-growth companies and define their behavior. On the other hand, big corporations emphasize strategy, structure, and process—institutionalizing corporate behavior patterns. They use chain-of-command management and consensus decision-making to reduce risk at the cost of timely action. Since the operating styles of an entrepreneurial company are so different from that of a large corporation, a marriage can be difficult.

The only way to improve the probability of a successful merger is for both parties to acknowledge the differences up front; clearly define goals and expectations; jointly devise the integration plan; provide adequate funding for growth; build in flexibility for unplanned surprises; and maintain a joint stake in the long-term success of the combination. In short, when a big corporation buys a small entrepreneurial company, both parties need to protect and incubate the unique ingredients that made the marriage so attractive in the first place. This is hard work that takes time, dedication, and investment.

## Some Marital Advice for Corporations

If you are planning to acquire an entrepreneurial venture to transform your business, you need to be prepared to accept, nurture, and adopt change. These changes can impact product innovation, technology applications, management practices, and financial performance. If you are not prepared to sponsor the transformation, then why make the acquisition? Let's face it; integrating an entrepreneurial company into an established corporate culture requires dedicated leadership and a willingness to face the stiff wind of resistance.

Rules to consider for acquiring and successfully on-boarding an entrepreneurial venture:

- Clearly define your goals and objectives for the acquisition.

- Secure line management buy-in before pursuing the target.

- Only make the acquisition if you are committed to genuine change.

- Invest the time up front to create a fertile environment for incubation.

- Be prepared to sponsor the integration up and down the organization.

- Make a covenant to preserve the ingredients of the secret sauce.

- Recognize that legacy practices aren't necessarily best practices.

- Study your acquisition for revolutionary methods and ideas.

- Nurture entrepreneurial leadership to foster change management.

- Recognize and reward a demonstrated commitment to transformation.

> And above all, do not acquire an
> entrepreneurial company for a quick fix.
> It just won't work.

## Some Marital Advice for Entrepreneurs

If you are considering the sale of your company to a large corporation, you will need to come to terms with the loss of control. This is a huge issue to digest. Just think about it: All of your success and behavior have been driven by your willingness to lead, to decide, and to take risks. You need to understand that your privileges and your autonomy will be affected by the new corporate owner. Coming to terms with this loss of freedom and empowerment can be very difficult and quite possibly insurmountable.

Having spent my first nine years in business with IBM and Hewlett-Packard, I had the advantage of understanding the motivation, behavior, and control issues within a large corporation. This background softened my conversion from entrepreneur to corporate executive. Yet even with this experience, my transition from USI to JCI proved very challenging. You should not underestimate the amount of change and loss of control you will be facing in the sale of your venture to a large corporation.

Beyond loss of control, your new corporate owner will hold you responsible to produce consistent results on a monthly, quarterly, and annual basis. You will also be responsible for facilitating a successful integration while achieving synergistic goals that bolster financial performance. Recognizing these new accountabilities should heighten your sensitivity to preserving your secret sauce—the key ingredients that make your company great.

# REMEMBER TO THINK BEYOND THE SALE

You need to take responsibility to negotiate the following post-sale operating terms into the final purchase and sale agreement:

- Preservation of vital ingredients in the secret sauce
- Clarity on reporting structure and responsibility
- Scope of decision-making authority
- Definition of spending latitude and constraints
- Control over recruiting and hiring
- Influence on compensation and reward decisions
- Input on integration time frame & budget
- Authority over business plan & implementation

# Epilogue

## TO THINE OWN SELF BE TRUE

One of my mother's favorite pieces of advice came from Polonius's speech to Laertes in Shakespeare's *Hamlet*, "To thine own self be true." As I approached the completion of my two-and-one-half-year contract term as CEO of JCI's Global Workplace Business for the Americas, I found myself reflecting on my mother's sage advice.

Even though JCI asked me to extend my contract and acknowledged my contributions with an Outstanding Leadership Award, I just knew I was an entrepreneur at heart. I missed the creativity, speed, and flexibility inherent in a smaller, more nimble organization. And I longed for the freedom to make the decisions without seeking permission. I met with JCI senior executives in July of 2007 to advise them that I would be departing at the end of December.

Once I made the decision to leave, I started to plan my next venture. I formed my new company, Blue Sunsets LLC, in November

2007 with liftoff scheduled for January 1, 2008—the day after my departure from Johnson Controls. Today, Blue Sunsets invests in small businesses, develops real estate projects, works with entrepreneurs, and provides intrapreneurship consulting to corporations (www.BlueSunsets.com).

## WORKING WITH ENTREPRENEURS

After departing Johnson Controls, a respected friend encouraged me to share my experience in the classroom. I considered the idea but could not picture myself in a full-time teaching role. Yet, I wanted to find a way to convey my knowledge to aspiring entrepreneurs. Since one of my life goals was to write a book, I realized that crafting a manuscript on entrepreneurship would enable me to achieve both objectives.

Over the course of the past three years, Wyn Lydecker and I have been pouring our collective knowledge and research into this project. Simultaneously, our social media director, Mary Jo Krump, has helped us open the pathway to the global entrepreneurship movement. Based on our interactions, it is clear that the pursuit of entrepreneurship and new business formation is truly a worldwide phenomenon.

Building bridges with aspiring entrepreneurs around the globe has been one of the most rewarding benefits of this endeavor. Every day, we find ourselves coaching, advising, and guiding entrepreneurs on the way forward in fulfilling their dreams.

More recently, we have taken our message on the road, scheduling speaking engagements, webinars, and podcasts with all types of entrepreneurs. Please let us know how we can help you with your entrepreneurial journey.

# THE

# STARTUP

# ROADMAP

ED "SKIP" McLAUGHLIN

WYN LYDECKER

PAUL McLAUGHLIN

# CONTENTS

# ABOUT THE STARTUP ROADMAP

The *Startup Roadmap* was designed with one purpose in mind: to improve your probability of startup success. The Roadmap is a step-by-step guide designed to help you understand the mechanics of starting and running a profitable new business.

Please feel free to contact us with questions and recommendations for improvement. We can be reached via email at: ed@thepurposeisprofit.com.

If you believe *The Startup Roadmap* can help your friends fulfill their entrepreneurial goals, please recommend it to them.

We wish you success in building your business. Please let us know how you are doing.

Sincerely,
Ed, Wyn, and Paul
www.thepurposeisprofit.com

# THE STARTUP ROADMAP

You know you want to start a business, but you are not sure how to do it. Like many entrepreneurs, you are chomping at the bit to lift off, but you are struggling with a healthy fear of failure. You need a step-by-step process to guide you through the uncertainties of starting up. If you are determined to build, lead, and grow a profitable business, *The Startup Roadmap* is designed for you.

You need a way to filter your ideas and figure out if they are bankable, sustainable, and worthy of your time, money, and reputation. You want to get started, but you do not want to take unnecessary risks. As much as possible, you want to look ahead and figure things out before you take the plunge—but you do not want to lose momentum, hamper your creativity, your energy, or your enthusiasm to get started—for fear you never will.

As I see it, you have a choice. You can invest the time up front to plan your journey, or you can roll the dice and launch without a plan, figuring out the inevitable problems and challenges as they present themselves. While I understand the need to pivot and make adjustments as you develop your business, I am not as confident in the concept of repeatedly trying, failing, and restarting, given the risks and costs to your livelihood. I believe you need to think through the essential steps to profitability before you launch.

A study by Harvard Business School senior lecturer Shikhar Ghosh showed that 75 percent of venture capital-backed startups fail and that non-venture capital-backed businesses fail at an even greater rate. To improve your probability of success, you need a means for exploring, testing, and validating ideas—one that builds your confidence that you are moving in the right direction before you start up. That's why I have developed *The Startup Roadmap.*

When I created the plans to launch my own business, USI, I followed a similar process. I could not afford to fail. I had a young family that relied on my income. Even though I couldn't wait to go out on my own, I had to consider the ramifications of leaving my corporate job. Prior to liftoff, my team and I invested six months of our time—without compensation—in careful speculation, answering the 21 questions included in *The Startup Roadmap.* It paid big dividends. We grew USI into an Inc. 500 company and then sold it 14 years later to Johnson Controls, a Fortune 100 company.

I want to share this Roadmap with you to help put you and your business on the path to long-term profit and success.

## 21 STEPS TO PROFITABILITY

The 21 steps in *The Startup Roadmap* fall into three categories: Proof, Profit, and Potential. First, you need to develop and prove your idea. Second, you have to figure out if you can make a profit. And third, you need to assess the business's potential for growth.

# SECTION

# 1

---

# PROOF

## Step 1

**Business Idea:** Can you state your business idea clearly and concisely?

If you cannot reduce your idea to a few simple, understandable sentences, then it may be too complex. And it will certainly be too hard to explain to potential customers, partners, and investors.

Before I launched, I talked to prospective customers and advisors to test and explain my business concept. I boiled down my idea into a single summary sentence: "We will become a corporation's single source of management for all their real estate needs." A corporation could outsource their entire real estate department to my new business, USI. Even though it was a novel concept, it clicked with my stakeholders right away.

To develop and hone your business idea, ask yourself the following questions:

- Why are you starting this business?

- What is the purpose of your new business?

- What product or service will you deliver?

- How is your business different?

- Will your stakeholders easily understand your idea?

A clear, crisp, and concise description of your business will help you acquire customers and build your brand.

## Step 2

**Distinctive Competence:** What unique experience, skills, and knowledge do you bring to your business?

If you can identify an unserved need for a product or service in an industry where you have distinctive competence, you could have a bankable business. You could minimize the risks by utilizing your knowledge of existing models, customers, customer needs, pricing, and competition.

I struggled for years pondering the type of business to start, its potential for profit, and the cost of possible failure. I thought through hundreds of scenarios and the associated risks, when one day, it struck me: The answer to all of these questions was distinctive competence.

When I looked back on my past successes, they had one thing in common: I had some combination of tried-and-true experience and a track record of accomplishment that enabled me to succeed. This mixture of experience and expertise defined my distinctive competence. I believed that if I built my new business around my distinctive competence I could substantially improve the probability of future success. The same principles apply to you.

If you believe you have a breakthrough business idea, then you will need the experience and the expertise to execute it. If you do not possess the necessary knowledge or skill to carry out your idea, you will need to hire or partner with someone who does.

Answer the following questions to determine your unique competence:

- What special knowledge, talent, or skill do you have?
- Do you have a track record of success in a particular field?
- How can you apply your talent to your new business?
- What additional competencies do you need to succeed?
- How can you fill the competency void with partners, team members, technology, tools, and/or education?

Challenging yourself to answer these questions will fortify your startup success.

## Step 3

**Product Description:** Can you succinctly describe the product you will sell, who will use it, and the problem it will solve?

It is critical to be able to articulate your product's features, its position in the marketplace, and its competitive advantage.

Traditionally, real estate transactions were handled entirely by local brokers, individual deal by individual deal. The market needed a more efficient process to get work done. Outsourcing was the answer. USI described its service as the outsourced manager of a corporation's real estate portfolio. USI became the customer's single point of contact for all their transaction and information needs. We promised to reduce occupancy costs, while rebating a share of the commissions to offset overall service delivery expenses. We hadn't thought of every service we could offer from the beginning, but we had a vision for selling a full suite of integrated services.

When starting out, you need to focus on the basics of your product's attributes, its position in the marketplace, and its profit potential, while keeping your ultimate vision in mind.

Answer the following questions to help develop your product description:

- What is your product or service?

- How will it be used, and who will use it?

- What problem will your product solve?

- What are your product's features?

- How is your product positioned in the market?

- What are your product's competitive advantages?

- How will your product evolve?

- Will you be offering a family of integrated products?

A clear and concise product description will enhance sales, improve product development, and create a platform for future product offerings.

# Step 4

**Market Opportunity:** What industry are you entering, and what are its trends?

Define the industry and the segment you will target. Recognize that the greatest opportunities lie in industry sectors that are growing and changing.

In my case, corporate real estate was undergoing dramatic change, creating significant opportunity. The mantra of the day was: Do more with less. The practice of outsourcing noncore service areas was beginning to take off. Corporations were saving millions by hiring outsourced providers with specialized expertise to reduce costs, enhance productivity, and improve service to customers.

My idea was to provide a service that would lead the outsourcing wave in corporate real estate. My business would enable companies to outsource the management of their real estate portfolios and a host of related services.

To define your market and the opportunity, you should invest the time to answer all of the following questions:

- What industry is your business in?
- What sector of the industry are you targeting?
- What changes are taking place?
- How does your product address the changes?
- How can your product create change?
- What is the size of the opportunity?
- What is the rate of growth of the target sector?
- What trends will impact the rate of growth?

Answering these questions may take some research. While you do the research, remember that it is important to stay at a high level. You don't want to get mired in minutiae. All of your answers should be available to you through online sources, industry groups, libraries, competitors, and business owners in the same sector.

## Step 5

**Target Customer:** Do you have a clear understanding of who will buy your product and why?

You need to be able to describe your target customer and their need for your product. You need to understand your customer's goals, motivations, budget, demographics, and characteristics, as well as their role and responsibility within the buying organization or household.

For USI, I knew my target customers were the chief financial officers (CFOs) and real estate executives (CREs) of corporations with substantial real estate holdings. They were in control of the budget and the real estate. Fortunately, I knew the industry inside and out, understood how it worked, and recognized what the CFOs and CREs were seeking. There was substantial opportunity for cost reduction and improved asset management. In most cases, real estate was—and still is—the second highest overhead expense, right after personnel costs.

Figure out how well you know your target customer by completing the following checklist:

- Who is the target customer for your product?
    - ○ Goals and motivations
    - ○ Demographic description
    - ○ Unique characteristics

- What is your customer's role and responsibility?
- Why does your customer need your product?
- What motivates your customer to buy your product?
- How does your customer influence the buying decision?
- Does your customer control the budget?
- How does your target customer measure success?

The best way to develop a profitable new business is through a comprehensive understanding of your target customer.

## Step 6

**Value Proposition:** What is your product's unique benefit, and how does that benefit meet a critical customer need?

The best value proposition clearly defines and quantifies how your product will solve a problem or relieve a customer's pain better than anything else.

The most efficient path to profit is a value proposition that succinctly explains the benefits and rewards your customer will derive from a relationship with your company. My experience has shown that a value proposition that provides a crystal-clear quantification of benefits is easiest to sell and the most compelling to buy. A business-to-business (B2B) value proposition is dominated by quantified benefits, whereas a business-to-consumer (B2C) value proposition leans more heavily on qualitative benefits.

When I was thinking about USI, I knew our value proposition would be our competitive differentiator. Since our competitors sold their products based on their brand names, using a traditional approach to sell and deliver their service, the doorway was wide open for change. I was confident we would have a bankable value proposition if we could demonstrate how our target customers could receive quantified benefits many times greater than the cost they paid. USI's value proposition was so well received that it propelled USI to a 40 percent compounded annual growth rate.

## Define Quantitative Benefits (Typically B2B)

To develop your B2B value proposition and generate a clear picture of your quantitative benefits, you should answer the following questions.

How much can your product—

- Increase your customer's revenues?
- Decrease your customer's expenses?
- Contribute to your customer's profits?
- Improve your customer's productivity?
- Reduce your customer's cycle time?
- Improve your customer's supply chain?
- Improve access to critical information?

Once my partners and I nailed down the hard benefits of our product, we also enumerated the qualitative benefits, including higher quality service, improved employee morale, enhanced customer satisfaction, etc. You need to compile a list of both quantitative and qualitative benefits for your B2B product.

## Define Qualitative Benefits (Typically B2C)

To define your B2C product's benefit(s), ask questions that center on alleviating pain or providing a distinct advantage for your customer.

Narrow down your unique qualitative benefits by asking if your B2C product will do any of the following:

- Make life more convenient?
- Provide safety or security?
- Increase self-esteem or confidence?
- Improve the quality of life?
- Improve health?

Once you determine and describe your product's qualitative benefits, you should also specify the quantitative benefits of your B2C product, such as saving time and money.

# Step 7

**Competitive Advantage:** What differentiates your business from the competition?

You can identify your competitive advantage by comparing and contrasting your value proposition against the value propositions of your finest competitors. This process will set your business apart by pinpointing the genuine elements of differentiation between you and your competitors.

Your competitive differentiation can come from any number of sources. USI had a multifaceted competitive advantage. Even though I knew I would be competing with my former employer, I intended to go after a different segment of the market. My former employer focused on the Fortune 100, while USI would target the middle of the Fortune 1000. In our market segment, we had the first-mover advantage with a sustainable, innovative business model: a new way for corporations to manage their real estate portfolios through outsourcing.

Based on your competitive research, you should be able to generate a list of your competitors, along with their value propositions. This information will give you a picture of the competitive landscape, allowing you to identify your truly unique advantages.

You can identify your competitive advantage by completing the following steps:

1. List your competitors and their value propositions.

2. Compare your value proposition to your competitors'.

3. Answer the following questions to determine your unique advantages vs. those of your competition:

   a. Does your product fill a gap in the market?

   b. Do you have a first-mover advantage?

   c. Is your product innovative?

   d. Is your product disruptive vis-à-vis traditional models?

   e. Are you using technology as a competitive weapon?

   f. Do you have control of your intellectual property?

   g. Do you have a unique talent or special reputation?

   h. Does your product improve customer productivity?

   i. Does your product increase customer revenues?

   j. Does your product save your customer money?

4. Determine if your competitive advantage is sustainable.

Pinpointing your competitive differentiation will crystallize your genuine advantages in comparison to the competition.

# Step 8

**Preorders:** Can you secure preorders from your target customers?

A preorder is an informal commitment from customers to purchase your product before it is formally offered to the market. Preorders are vital to any new business because they validate your business idea before you launch.

Like many entrepreneurs forming B2B startups, I had the advantage of a significant, preexisting corporate relationship base to build on. My reputation put me well ahead of the game in lining up preorders. In a few cases, my customer relationships were close enough that I could try out my idea informally. It turned out that this would be the way I would secure my first preorders. That gave me the confidence to leave my job and launch my business. Looking back, I realize that my preorders were the key factor that led to achieving profitability in USI's fourth month of operation.

Securing presales is the single most important point of validation and vitality for a new business. If you can line up enough preorders, you can maximize control of your company and minimize the need for outside funding.

To secure preorders, you should do the following:

- Generate a target list of high-trust contacts and likely buyers of your new product.

- Internalize your value proposition and be able to articulate it clearly and concisely when you meet with prospects.

- Contact your closest customers—ones whom you trust—and ask them if they would place an order with your startup.

- Approach trusted advisors and ask them to make introductions to prospective customers.

- Sell your competitive advantages to clearly delineate your product in the mind of your customer.

- Close for the preorder and document the commitment to do business together.

Secure as many preorders as you can reasonably fill on time, on budget, and at the quality level your customer expects. Keep in mind that your reputation for fulfilling your commitments is your number one asset.

# 2

# PROFIT

## Step 9

**Business Model:** How will you make money?

The business model explains how you will pull together and manage all the component parts of your business to create value for your customers and yourself. Your business model includes your revenue generation plan, product pricing, production and distribution, use of technology, marketing and sales, resource requirements, and profit validation.

Too often entrepreneurs fall in love with their idea but fail to have a business model worked out that will make a profit and generate sustainable cash flow.

When I worked at Trammell Crow Company, the vice president of real estate at Baxter Healthcare and I developed the business engine to outsource hundreds of transactions and construction projects. This was the first time real estate services were outsourced. The concept was completely innovative. Because I had worked so intimately on developing the business model, I knew the math involved and felt certain of the huge profit potential a similar model could generate for a new outsourcing business.

The Profit section of *The Startup Roadmap* includes the eight major components of the business model. These components are listed below and discussed in detail in Steps 10 through 17.

*Step 10:* Revenue Generation

*Step 11:* Product Pricing

*Step 12:* Production & Distribution

*Step 13:* Creative Use of Technology

*Step 14:* Marketing

*Step 15:* Sales

*Step 16:* Resource Requirements

*Step 17:* Profit Validation

Please do not underestimate the importance of a sound business model and all of its component parts to your ability to create value and generate profit.

# Step 10

**Revenue Generation:** How will you generate revenue?

A key step in developing your revenue model is determining the types and sources of revenue your business will generate. Revenue types include product sales, service fees, advertising sales, data access fees, license fees, and/or commissions.

Each type of revenue generated can come from a multitude of sources. For example, sources of revenue from service sales can vary depending on customer type and category, including online, mobile, consumer, corporate, institutional, and/or government. Additionally, each category can expand into multiple sources. For example, the corporate sales category can include major accounts, named accounts, vertical markets, geographic territories, partnerships, and one-off sales.

USI had a pretty simple revenue model. We sold real estate portfolio management and transaction management services to corporations. Our customers paid us fees for dedicated resources and commissions on transactions. As the business evolved and our service lines expanded, we developed a more complex fee structure suited to the types of services our customers consumed.

How will you structure your revenue model?

- Will you collect sales revenue directly from customers in exchange for the service or product?

- Will your business act as an intermediary, helping to bring buyers and sellers together and collecting a fee for the service or a commission on the resulting sale?

- Will your business be a publisher of content or the creator of an online community that charges for access to the content or community?

- Will you provide content or community for free and collect revenues from advertisers who want to target your readers or users?

- Will you give permission for your product to be used in exchange for a license fee?

- Will you be a collector of data and charge fees to marketers for access to that information?

- Will your business use a combination of these revenue models?

Determining the types and sources of revenue your business will generate is the first step toward realizing a profit.

# Step 11

**Product Pricing:** What will you charge for your product?

Determine your price by selecting your revenue model while factoring in your competitive positioning and your ideal profit target. Each type of revenue model will most likely have market benchmarks you can research to help you price competitively.

From my previous corporate sales experience, I had a firm understanding of traditional pricing models for real estate services. By aggregating portfolio and transaction services through a single source, I knew I could cover my costs and beat the competition with aggressive volume-based pricing. If you know your industry, you may be able to do the same.

Consider the following questions:

- Will you be developing a radical new pricing model?

- Will your price be aligned with traditional benchmarks?

- Will your price be competitive?

- Will you be selling a premium product, enabling you to charge more than your competitors, or will you undercut the competition?

- Should you use a simple markup to cover your unit costs?

- If you are a content provider, what are the prevailing rates for the type of advertising you are selling?

- If you are a provider of data, what do marketers typically pay for access to similar information?

- Will your price cover your cost and leave room for a reasonable profit?

Once you can explain the basic revenue model and your pricing, you can estimate how many customers you expect to have, how many sales you'll likely make to each one, and how often you will make those sales—daily, weekly, monthly, or annually. Taken together, this information will enable you to project your total revenue.

## Step 12

**Production and Distribution:** What will it take to create, manufacture, and deliver your product to your customers?

For a manufactured product, you will need to think through and quantify your requirements for raw materials, labor, machinery, inventory, and distribution. For a service business, you will need to quantify your service fulfillment costs including staffing, travel costs, response times, and performance reporting.

Since USI was a service business, we were concerned about sales and service delivery costs. Beyond the production of proposals and due-diligence binders, we did not have a manufacturing cost. The key components of our product were account management, data management, market knowledge, and negotiation skills. USI's expenses were very similar to a traditional consulting business, with most of our employees situated on-site at our customers' headquarters.

On the other hand, a manufacturing and distribution business has a more significant challenge in accurately estimating production costs. It will be important to develop a thorough production cost model to ensure you have considered all of the major costs.

Some of the factors you will need to address to estimate production costs include the following:

### Prototype costs

- How will you create a prototype or samples to help you secure preorders?

- How much will it cost to create a prototype or sample products?

### Production costs

- Quantify the type, amount, and source of materials, labor, and equipment needed to manufacture your product.

- Generate a preliminary estimate of costs for materials, labor, and/or equipment needed for your product.

- Determine whether you will make your product or outsource its production.

- If you make your product,
  - What are your raw material costs?
  - What are your labor costs?
  - What are your equipment costs?
  - What are your facilities costs?
  - What are your distribution costs?
  - How long will it take to manufacture your product?

- What is the total unit production cost of your product?

- If you outsource, who will make your product, how much will it cost, and how long will it take?
- Finalize the make vs. buy decision by weighing the quantitative and qualitative benefits of each.

Determining accurate production costs and time frames for a manufacturing business is critical to the development of a profitable and reliable business model. Please keep in mind that this is merely a high-level outline designed to get you started.

# Step 13

**Creative Use of Technology:** How will you leverage technology to streamline your operations, improve customer service, and open up new revenue lines?

Intelligent use of technology can create a distinct competitive advantage, tighten your relationship with customers, improve access to critical information, and generate a recurring profit stream.

When I was thinking through my business model, I planned on applying my high-tech background from my early career at both IBM and HP to the low-tech world of real estate. I understood the value of systems integration and believed that a similar approach could be used to manage the incredible variety of information and relationships within corporate real estate. Systems integration turned out to be a distinguishing characteristic of our business model, ultimately creating a new service sector that opened the door for USI to offer even more benefits to our customers.

We developed a proprietary software solution named Sequentra to serve the corporate real estate market. We created a wholly separate brand and housed it within a new company named Sequentra Solutions Inc. We used Sequentra as one of our strategic weapons. Our software enabled workflows, improved access to critical information, and tightened our link with the customer.

Here are some of the questions you should consider when applying technology to your business:

- How can you utilize technology to differentiate your offering?

- How can you develop software applications that provide critical decision support information and new revenue streams?

- How can you apply technology to streamline work processes?

- How can you utilize technology to tighten the link with your customers?

- How can you utilize technology to create a sustainable competitive advantage?

- How can you utilize technology to revolutionize your industry?

Today, the technology platforms available are growing exponentially, and with them, the opportunities to create businesses of incredible lasting value. If you are not the tech person in your business, make sure you invest in finding a good one.

## Step 14

**Marketing:** How will you create awareness and persuade customers to buy your product?

As a startup, you need a plan to reach and educate your target customers about the benefits of your value proposition without spending a lot of money. Establish a meaningful budget, implement your marketing plan, and measure your plan based on tangible results.

Successful marketing depends upon determining the most cost-effective means to communicate your value proposition to your target customer. Since we had a finite list of target customers—the CFOs and CREs of the Fortune 1000—we decided the best way to motivate interest in our company was to communicate a consistent message of success. The primary goal of our early marketing efforts was to create a receptive audience for our sales force.

First, we needed to notify our target market that we existed—by announcing the formation and purpose of USI. Second, we had to raise awareness of our value proposition—especially how we were different from our competitors. Third, we needed to bombard our target market with consistent monthly announcements of our achievements. We wanted our target audience to feel as though they were missing something of value if they did not meet with us.

Since we had a finite audience, we needed point-to-point marketing, not mass media. At the time, we used direct mail. Nowadays, we would develop a targeted email campaign, supplemented with social media, all connected through a closed-loop system utilizing our website and mobile applications.

Successful businesses connect with their customers on multiple levels and in numerous dimensions, the scope of which is subject to cost constraints.

The following components should be part of your marketing mix:

- Website
- Online advertising
- Social media
- Mobile
- Direct email
- Promotions
- Collateral package
- Events
- Public relations
- CRM systems

When putting your marketing plan together, it's important to remember that everything should flow from your value proposition. You cannot develop an effective marketing plan unless you know your target customer, their needs, and how your product satisfies their needs.

Some of the most important questions you should address in your marketing plan include the following:

1. What are the most cost-effective ways to build awareness of your new venture with your target customers?

2. How can you communicate your value proposition to your target customers?

3. How can you secure permission from your target customers to utilize their email addresses for direct marketing?

4. How can you design a cost-effective, unobtrusive way to keep your target customer informed of your success?

5. How can you persuade and influence your target customer to buy from you?

Be careful not to undervalue the role of marketing in your startup. You have made a decision to start a new company, and you are confident in your value proposition. Make sure your target customers know that you exist and educate them on the benefits of your value proposition.

# Step 15

**Sales:** How will you secure hard orders from your target customers?

Your sales team is responsible for connecting directly with the customer for the purpose of solving problems, tailoring solutions, making proposals, and closing orders. Will you build a direct sales force, develop a call center, create an e-commerce platform, or outsource the sales function? You need to determine the most efficient path for securing sales.

At USI we recognized the importance of developing face-to-face customer relationships for real estate outsourcing services. Our direct sales force was one of the keys to our long-term success. Since the salesperson was the direct link to our target customer, USI invested in recruiting the best talent to build our sales team. We became a sales-driven company and built a sales platform responsible for all of the following activities:

- Developing and pursuing sales leads

- Separating qualified buyers from window shoppers

- Developing sales tools and tailored presentations

- Conducting sales meetings with target customers

- Generating preemptive proposals

- Responding to requests for proposals (RFPs)

- Finding solutions to complex customer problems

- Signing contracts and closing sales

- Continuously updating the customer relationship management (CRM) system

- Building deep customer relationships

- Influencing new product development

- Developing exclusive multiyear contracts

Your product will not sell itself. Investing in a sales platform tailored to your product is vital to your success. The sales platform you select will be influenced by the complexity of the sale, the amount of product customization required, customer buying habits, and competitive sales methods.

Building an effective sales platform contoured to your business goals is expensive and time consuming, but critically important. There are no shortcuts. Since your sales platform is the face of your organization to your target customer, you need to get it right.

# Step 16

**Resource Requirements:** What will it take to develop, produce, distribute, and sell your product?

Generate a comprehensive list of all the resources needed to enable successful liftoff and ongoing operations. Quantify the cost of all the required resources, including human, material, equipment, space, services, and capital needs. Having this information will help you figure out what it will cost to launch and operate your business.

For USI, I knew the business model, how to implement it, and how to sell it. But I needed people to help me execute the work and manage the business. I also needed office space, equipment, and trusted professionals to advise me. I could estimate these costs pretty easily.

When you boil it down, most businesses do three things: source, execute, and manage. Utilizing this three-step format will help you quantify your resource requirements.

## Sourcing New Business

- How many sales people do you need to develop new business?

- How much will it cost in travel, materials, salary, commissions, and overhead to develop new business?

## Executing Orders

- How many people do you need to produce your product or deliver your service? Will you hire direct staff or contract with an outsource provider?

- For a manufacturing business, how much will it cost to produce your product in terms of raw materials, equipment, storage, distribution, salary, and overhead?

- For a service business, how much will it cost to deliver your service in terms of travel, materials, salary, and overhead?

- For a technology business, how much will it cost to deliver your service in terms of hardware, software, networks, salary, and overhead?

## Managing the Business

- How many people do you need to manage, plan, and direct the business? What will your management team cost in salary and overhead?

- How many people do you need to administer the business? What will your administrative resources cost in salary and overhead?

- How much infrastructure do you need? What will you spend on space, furniture, office equipment, communications, etc.?

- How much money will you need for professional services such as legal, accounting, insurance, banking, and consultants?

Although this methodology is not exhaustive, it does provide a simple framework to quantify resource requirements and costs for business liftoff and ongoing operations.

# Step 17

**Profit Validation:** Can you forecast a profit? Simple, back-of-an-envelope calculations will demonstrate if your business model can generate a profit.

The basics of making a profit come down to this simple formula:

### revenues − expenses = profit (or loss)

You can validate annual profit or loss by completing the following calculation:

- Projected revenues (average sale × projected number of annual sales) minus
- Projected cost of revenue (average cost of sale × projected number of annual sales) minus
- Overhead expenses equals
- Operating profit (or loss).

Since the primary revenue generator for USI was based on transaction fees, all I needed to do was project the number of real estate transactions that I could complete in my first year multiplied by an average transaction fee (20 transactions × $12,000 fee = $240,000 projected revenue).

For expenses, I estimated an average delivery cost for each transaction ($5,000 average delivery cost × 20 transactions = $100,000 projected expenses).

As a result, I calculated $240,000 revenue—$100,000 expenses would equal a gross profit of $140,000 in our first year.

I planned to control my overhead costs by eliminating my first year's salary, paying my partners with a combination of equity and a minimal salary, prepaying a low-cost sublease that included furniture and equipment, and putting a cap on travel expenses. Taken together, I estimated that we would run up $80,000 in overhead expenses in our first year. By subtracting our overhead expenses from our gross profit, we were able to project an operating profit of $60,000. In actuality, we generated an operating profit of almost $200,000 in our first year.

Validating your profit potential is a quick test of business viability. It can also help you identify and resolve problems or motivate startup actions. Here is how our simple projections looked:

**United Systems Integrators Corporation (USI)**
**Financial Projections (3 Years)**

|  | Year 1 | Year 2 | Year 3 |
|---|---|---|---|
| **Revenues** | $ 240,000 | $ 960,000 | $ 1,920,000 |
| Cost of Revenues | 100,000 | 400,000 | 800,000 |
| **Gross Profit** | 140,000 | 560,000 | 1,120,000 |
|  |  |  |  |
| Overhead Expenses |  |  |  |
| Salaries and Benefits | 60,000 | 240,000 | 480,000 |
| Sales and Marketing | 10,000 | 40,000 | 80,000 |
| General and Administrative | 10,000 | 40,000 | 80,000 |
| Research and Development | - | - | - |
| **Total Overhead Expenses** | 80,000 | 320,000 | 640,000 |
| Depreciation & Amortization | - | - | - |
| **Total Expenses** | 80,000 | 320,000 | 640,000 |
|  |  |  |  |
| **Operating Profit** | $ 60,000 | $ 240,000 | $ 480,000 |
| Interest & Taxes | 6,000 | 48,000 | 120,000 |
| **Net Profit (Loss)** | $ 54,000 | $ 192,000 | $ 360,000 |

*USI financial projections*

# 3

## POTENTIAL

## Step 18

**Financial Projections:** How will you know when you will make a profit?

This is the point when you need to calculate more detailed, month-by-month estimates of how much you can sell, when you will sell it, and what you will charge. You also need to figure out the direct cost of generating your sales, and your total overhead expenses, on a more granular basis for at least the first year of operations or until you reach breakeven. These projections will show you when you will generate a profit.

Rather than USI's service-based model, let's take a look at a product-based model to broaden the variables that impact financial projections.

## Methodology for Estimating Profit

**Let's talk about costs first.** The terms *expenses* and *costs* can be used interchangeably, and there are two types: direct and indirect. Try not to get hung up on details that can be addressed later. You will miss the mark if you overinvest your time in this exercise. Let me give you an example of how simple your calculations can be.

*First,* you should figure out your direct costs or cost of revenues (also known as cost of goods sold). What will your product cost to produce and distribute?

*Second,* you should figure out your indirect costs or overhead expenses. What are your management and sales costs? Refer to Step 16: Resource Requirements for greater detail.

Remember, at this stage all you need are rough estimates that you can put into a spreadsheet.

### Estimate Unit Costs

After some quick research, you determine that the product will cost $70 per unit to produce and $30 per unit to distribute—or $100 total direct cost per unit (cpu).

### Estimate Product Sales

Now that you've estimated your direct unit costs, it's time to tackle how many units you believe you will sell. These estimates affect both your direct costs and your revenues. You can think in terms of the number of units, but you also need to specify a time period. How many units can you sell daily, weekly, monthly, or annually? For example, I believe that I can sell 50 units per week or 200 units per month or 2,400 units per year in my first year of operation.

Then, let's calculate the total direct costs: $100 direct cost per unit × 2,400 units per year = $240,000 annual direct costs.

## Price Your Product and Estimate Revenues

Since units sold × price = revenues, you will need to determine the price you will charge for your product. For now, just look at two options: cost-plus or market price. Both of these options can be influenced by your product's value to the customer and what customers pay for similar products from competitors.

To calculate cost-plus pricing, figure that a typical markup for a high-value product can range from 50% to 100% (or substantially more for premium products). For this example, let's use assume a 60% markup to determine the price under a cost-plus model: $100 total cpu + 60% markup = $160 price per unit.

## Estimate Your Overhead

Using your resource requirements estimate, you need to add up all your ongoing overhead costs including salaries and benefits; sales and marketing expenses; general and administrative expenses; and research and development. In our example, overhead expenses total $160,000 in the first year.

## Simple Calculations

Now, you can figure out the total annual operating profit. Start by estimating revenues:

**price per unit × units sold per year = estimated revenues**

In our example, $160 price per unit × 2,400 units per year = $384,000 in total estimated revenues. Next, we should calculate total direct costs:

### cost per unit (production + distribution costs) × units per year = total direct costs

In our example, we have $100 cost per unit × 2,400 units per year = $240,000 total direct costs. The difference between the revenues and direct costs (or cost of revenues) is your gross profit:

### revenue − direct cost = gross profit

In our example, $384,000 in annual revenues − $240,000 in annual costs = $144,000 in annual gross profit. From there, you can determine if your gross profit covers your indirect (or overhead) costs:

### gross profit − indirect costs = operating profit (loss)

In our example, $144,000 is gross profit minus $160,000 in total overhead expenses minus $8,000 in depreciation and amortization = ($24,000) operating loss. Unlike a service business with minimal direct costs, a product business has substantial direct costs. However, once the revenue engine ramps up and overhead stabilizes, a manufacturing business can generate substantial profits.

Here is how the three-year projections for the manufacturing business in our example look:

**Manufacturing Startup**
**Financial Projections (3 Years)**

| | Year 1 | Year 2 | Year 3 |
|---|---|---|---|
| **Revenues** | $ 384,000 | $ 1,152,000 | $ 3,456,000 |
| Cost of Revenues | 240,000 | 720,000 | 2,160,000 |
| **Gross Profit** | 144,000 | 432,000 | 1,296,000 |
| | | | |
| Overhead Expenses | | | |
| Salaries and Benefits | 100,000 | 200,000 | 600,000 |
| Sales and Marketing | 20,000 | 40,000 | 120,000 |
| General and Administrative | 30,000 | 60,000 | 180,000 |
| Research and Development | 10,000 | 20,000 | 60,000 |
| **Total Overhead Expenses** | 160,000 | 320,000 | 960,000 |
| Depreciation & Amortization | 8,000 | 12,000 | 16,000 |
| Total Expenses | 168,000 | 332,000 | 976,000 |
| | | | |
| **Operating Profit** | (24,000) | 100,000 | 320,000 |
| Interest & Taxes | - | 9,600 | 100,800 |
| **Net Profit (Loss)** | $ (24,000) | $ 90,400 | $ 219,200 |

*Manufacturing startup projections*

You will need to generate projections to make sure you can achieve your minimum profit objectives and to secure funding. To determine how your financial outlook will improve during your first year, fill out a spreadsheet on a month-by-month basis, using reasonable estimates for sales growth with proportional costs to support the growth.

Asking yourself if you can make a profit within your first 18 months of operation is a vital gut check that will help you make the decision whether or not to move forward. Exceptions include technology and biotech startups because of the amount of capital and extended time frames needed to reach profitability.

# Step 19

**Cash Flow:** Will you have enough cash?

Using your projections and estimates of your resource requirements, you can forecast how much cash you will spend monthly, commonly referred to as your monthly burn rate. Using best, likely, and worst-case scenarios, figure out the point at which the business will generate more cash than it burns. Use the results to understand how much cash to set aside to cover your expenses until you generate positive cash flow.

Even though I knew that any contracts USI would bring in could have big pay offs, I couldn't count on generating enough recurring revenue to cover all my operating costs up front. Because I was planning to bootstrap the business, I wanted to be very conservative so I would not worry about running out of cash while we ramped up. This forced me to figure out a worst-case scenario and set aside $100,000 of my own money to fund startup costs and any contingencies.

To get a handle on your cash needs, some of the questions to consider include:

- What will you spend before starting operations?

- What will it cost to launch?

- How much will you spend on creating a prototype or samples to generate presales?

- If you have to produce and store inventory before customers pay for it, how much will that cost?

- If you have to make a capital expenditure to purchase a plant or equipment, how much will it be?

- How fast will you burn through your cash?

- When will operating profits contribute to your
  bank account?

Having the answers to these questions before you launch will enable a successful liftoff. It doesn't matter if you're going to seek outside investors or if you are investing in yourself by bootstrapping; it's essential to have a handle on what it will take—and how long it will take—to turn the corner to profitability and achieve positive cash flow.

Keep in mind that operating cash flow is the key metric investors analyze to make funding decisions. Operating cash flow is also known as earnings before interest, taxes, depreciation, and amortization, or EBITDA.

## Step 20

**Management Team:** How will you manage your business?

Your startup will have lots of moving parts, requiring people with different types of expertise to fulfill your vision. Think through what you can do yourself, and then bring in a team with complementary skills to get the job done.

I knew I needed a team to help me launch and grow USI. I had learned over the years that teams tend to create more value than individuals. If you are intent on creating a scalable business, you'll quickly realize that you cannot do it by yourself. You will need to recruit and hire people whom you can trust, the kind of people who can help you strategize, innovate, execute, and—when things look their darkest—commiserate and overcome challenges together.

To decide who will be on your team, you should ask yourself these questions:

- Who will lead? Who will sell? Who will execute?
- What value or competence do you bring to the business?
- What will be your role and responsibility?
- What additional value or competence is needed?
- What roles and responsibilities need to be filled?
- Who will complement your operating style?
- Who will work with you 24/7 to fulfill the vision?

Then, ask yourself if you know people you can trust to fill the roles. If you cannot identify trusted partners, you will need to develop a personalized recruitment plan utilizing your network of trusted friends and associates.

## Step 21

**Future Growth:** How will you expand the business and
your bottom line?

Do you have a strategic vision for growth? Do you have a plan to scale the business? To realize the full potential of your business, you need to develop a viable expansion plan to increase revenues and profits.

USI provided a family of integrated real estate, management, and information services in response to customers' evolving outsourcing needs. Our growth strategy included customer relationship expansion, new service lines, new markets including global expansion, formation of specialized partnerships, and limited strategic acquisitions. All of the following strategies can contribute to your growth.

**Customer Growth**

- Expand existing customer accounts
- Establish account profit centers to drive growth
- Develop new customer accounts
- Provide credit to finance customer purchases

**Product Growth**

- Expand existing product lines
- Create new products and services
- Develop product bundles
- Establish product line profit centers

**Geographic Growth**

- Expand geographically to open new markets
- Establish geographic profit centers
- Develop global expansion plans

**Corporate Growth**

- Recruit and hire specialized leadership talent
- Create innovation centers
- Consider strategic partnerships
- Assess mergers and acquisitions

Your startup should be focused on survival, profitability, and cash flow. Once your business has been established, you can start to develop a strategic growth plan.

THE

# STARTUP FUNDING GUIDE

ED "SKIP" McLAUGHLIN

WYN LYDECKER

PAUL McLAUGHLIN

# THE STARTUP FUNDING GUIDE

Once you have decided to become an entrepreneur, you will need to decide how you will fund your new business. As discussed in chapter 5, capital, cost, and control are the primary variables that impact your choice of startup funding. In the process of securing your startup funding, you will need to complete the following steps:

1. Determine your funding requirements

2. Build your financial model
   a. Plan cash expenditures for assets
   b. Understand the impact of cash flow
   c. Develop your financial projections

3. Acknowledge the cost of capital: equity & debt

4. Develop and deliver your pitch

5. Understand the investor's point of view

6. Determine your source of funding

   a. Other people's money—equity or debt

   b. Your own money—bootstrapping

   c. Beyond friends, family, & banks

7. Make the right funding decision

## DETERMINING YOUR FUNDING REQUIREMENTS

Before you can decide whether you should seek outside capital or self-fund your business, you must have a clear understanding of how much funding you really need. Since outside capital is costly, you do not want to seek more funding than necessary. At the same time, you need to make sure you will have enough money to stay afloat until you achieve positive cash flow. Cash is the lifeblood of your business. As long as you have enough cash available, you can continue to operate.

To determine how much funding your new business requires, you will need to develop a comfort level with basic financial literacy. This section of our book, combined with chapter 5 and *The Startup Roadmap* (steps 9–19), will provide you with the early knowledge you need to develop and understand the financial model for your business.

When you show your financial model to investors or lenders, it will tell the story of your startup's potential. Investors want to know that you have done research and have carefully thought through the assumptions behind your model. If you are bootstrapping, your projections will help you determine how much of your savings you'll need to invest in your business.

The process of making reasonable estimates can be challenging. The best way to build reliable projections is to think through the worst-case and the best-case scenarios to arrive at the most realistic case. Walking through this process usually results in a reasonable and achievable model. By considering the outside parameters, you will have the confidence to develop the most-likely case.

## BUILDING YOUR FINANCIAL MODEL

To build your financial model, you will need to research, analyze, and estimate revenues and costs. When will your revenue stream begin? What will it look like? Will it grow slowly, quickly, smoothly, unevenly, seasonally, or exponentially?

If you have proven competence in the industry you are entering, then estimating your revenues (and your costs) should be familiar and straightforward. If you lack relevant experience, you can research industry benchmarks by interviewing potential customers, speaking with competitors, and contacting trade associations, or by reading research reports, press releases, and corporate SEC filings. When you draw up projections for an investor presentation, be sure to cite any sources you used to come up with your assumptions. Investors like to look at comparables. And it's valuable for you to analyze comparables just to be sure you're making reasonable estimates.

### Revenues

Start your projections by estimating how much you will charge for each unit and how many units of your product you believe you can sell at different time intervals—weekly, monthly, and annually. Use your assumptions to extrapolate your revenue projections.

**price per unit × units sold per year =
estimated revenues**

## Costs

Costs are just as important to estimate as revenues. In fact, some investors put more weight on realistic cost estimates than on aggressive revenue projections. It should come as no surprise that investors will be concerned about how fast you will burn through their cash. If you decide to self-fund and consume your own cash, you need to know how fast you will deplete your personal savings.

### Cost of Revenues and Gross Profit

Start by figuring out what it will cost to make and ship the number of units you plan to sell. For a manufacturing company, these expenses include your direct costs for raw materials, labor, warehousing, and shipping for each unit. For a service business, they include fulfillment costs such as dedicated resources, travel, and reporting. These amounts reflect what it will cost to deliver your product or service and are known as your cost of revenues or cost of goods sold.

**cost per unit (production + distribution costs) ×
units sold per year = cost of revenues**

The difference between your revenue and what it costs to generate that revenue is your gross profit.

**revenues − cost of revenues = gross profit**

Your gross profit divided by your revenues gives you your *gross profit margin*. It shows the percentage of sales revenue that can flow through the company to cover your overhead expenses and contribute to your bottom line. Lenders and investors look at gross margin to determine how well you are managing the costs of manufacturing your product or delivering your service in relation to the prices you charge. Gross margins vary dramatically by industry. For example, software companies tend to have gross margins of close to 90 percent, while retailers can have gross margins of close to 40 percent.

**gross profit / revenue = gross profit margin**

## Overhead Expenses and Breakeven

Once you understand your gross profits, then you need to figure out your *overhead expenses*. Typically, overhead expenses include salaries, benefits, rent, telecommunications, equipment, legal, accounting, insurance, travel, marketing, and other costs. You may have to do some research to make these estimates. To keep your overhead under control, ask yourself if you and your management team can work for little or no pay during the liftoff year, perhaps working only for an equity stake. Can you make do with a shared space or a warehouse rather than spending precious dollars on office rent? Any cost you can avoid at the beginning will help you achieve profitability faster. When your *gross profit* covers your *overhead costs*, you have reached your *breakeven point*.

### Cash Flow from Operations or EBITDA

When your gross profit exceeds your overhead, you will start generating positive cash flow from operations.

**gross profit − overhead expenses =
cash flow from operations**

Investors typically want to look at your cash flow from operations, also known as earnings before interest, taxes, depreciation, and amortization (EBITDA). By looking at your actual and projected operating cash flow, or EBITDA, investors will get a good idea of the current and future health of your business. It is important to keep in mind that operating cash flow is a key metric that many investors analyze in making funding decisions. At the same time, you should be aware that EBITDA is a non-GAAP (generally accepted accounting principles) measure and usually is not shown on financial statements.

Cash flow from operations is simply the cash you take in from sales and the cash you pay out to cover day-to-day expenses. Many things can affect your cash flow, such as how quickly you pay your bills or how fast your customers pay you. You will need to manage your cash flow if you want to have enough money to stay in business (more on this later).

### Operating Profit or EBIT

Because EBITDA is not usually shown on the income statement, the metric you will be calculating for your projections is *operating profit—or EBIT—Earnings Before Interest and Taxes.*

**gross profit − operating expenses =
operating profit**

## Net Profit

*Net profit* is what's left over after you pay any remaining expenses, such as interest payments and taxes.

**operating profit – interest & taxes = net profit**

Just as with your gross profit margin, you will need to keep a handle on your net profit margin. Your *net profit* divided by *sales revenues* gives you *net profit margin*. It's the percentage of the sales revenue that flows to the bottom line. By understanding your net profit margin, you can better manage your cash flow and profit. Typically, as a business grows and achieves economies of scale, it can increase its net profit margin. An increasing margin is a clear sign of a healthy business and a strong indication of a solid management team.

**net profit / sales revenue = net profit margin**

## Planning Cash Expenditures for Assets

When you are starting and running your business, you will have other expenditures that don't show up in profit and loss calculations. These expenditures will consume cash and will show up on your balance sheet as assets. Assets fall into two categories: current and long-term. Cash, inventory, and prepaid expenses are examples of current assets, whereas plant and equipment are examples of long-term assets.

It is important to note that your inventory will not generate a dime of revenue until it is sold. For example, a retail or manufacturing startup can consume a great deal of cash producing and stockpiling inventory long before it is sold to a customer. Overbuying and underselling inventory can tie up vital cash resources leading to increased failure rates. You need to plan to have enough cash on hand to cover the period before the sales are made and the payments collected. As previously referenced, the portion of inventory that you sell becomes the cost of revenues on your P&L.

Other purchases you make will become long-term assets. Typically, when you acquire assets that will be used to support your business over the long term, you will capitalize those expenditures. Capitalized assets are depreciated over a defined useful life as they are used to produce your products. The basic concept is that you are matching revenues to expenses over time. Some of the expenditures will be recurring, and some will be intermittent. When you are deciding how much startup funding you need, you should plan and quantify these expenditures.

By the way, the useful life of an asset should be calculated in conformance with current IRS regulations, as well as with GAAP. To ensure conformance, it is usually beneficial to seek the guidance of a Certified Public Accountant (CPA).

## Understanding the Impact of Cash Flow

As a startup, you will probably have negative cash flow because you are spending money on building your business before you have generated enough revenue to cover all the costs and expenditures you are making. Investors will ask you when you expect to become cash-flow positive. Once your business is generating positive cash flow, there will be less need for outside funding.

When you are forecasting how much funding you'll require, you need to look beyond cash flow from operations and keep in mind that you may have recurring expenditures that are not covered immediately by incoming cash. Your inventory may not sell for days or even months, lengthening your inventory turn rate. Your customers may take months to pay you, extending the time it takes to collect your receivables. In the meantime, your vendors will expect you to pay them. All this takes working capital and is a drain on cash. Some of the working capital needs can be covered by your profits. But you may also need to put in your own funds or secure financing from investors or lenders to have enough cash to stay open. Be sure to include these operating cycle expenditures in your funding calculations.

Believe it or not, a company can show a loss on its income statement but continue day-to-day operations as long as it has cash available. On the other hand, even when a company shows a net profit, if it runs out of cash, it will go out of business.

Even more important than positive cash flow is the generation of free cash flow. For an operating business, free cash flow is the amount of cash that can be withdrawn from the business and still leave the company with enough funds to operate. When a company enjoys free cash flow, it can pay down debt, invest in growth, or start to build up a cushion for emergencies.

## Developing Your Financial Projections

All of these financial metrics influence funding decisions. In order to obtain funding, you will need to generate an income statement and a balance sheet. In certain instances, you may also be required to produce a statement of cash flows and/or a sources and uses of funds statement. The income statement for a startup is the most important projection.

The income statement should include the following:

- Revenues
- Cost of revenues

- Gross profit

- Overhead expenses

- Depreciation and amortization

- Operating profit or EBIT

- Interest & taxes

- Net profit

As an example, here is the income statement for my startup, USI. As a service business, we were able to achieve profitability in our first year of operation.

| United Systems Integrators Corporation (USI) Financial Projections (3 Years) | | | |
|---|---|---|---|
| | Year 1 | Year 2 | Year 3 |
| Revenues | $ 240,000 | $ 960,000 | $ 1,920,000 |
| Cost of Revenues | 100,000 | 400,000 | 800,000 |
| Gross Profit | 140,000 | 560,000 | 1,120,000 |
| | | | |
| Overhead Expenses | | | |
| Salaries and Benefits | 60,000 | 240,000 | 480,000 |
| Sales and Marketing | 10,000 | 40,000 | 80,000 |
| General and Administrative | 10,000 | 40,000 | 80,000 |
| Research and Development | - | - | - |
| Total Overhead Expenses | 80,000 | 320,000 | 640,000 |
| Depreciation & Amortization | - | - | - |
| Total Expenses | 80,000 | 320,000 | 640,000 |
| | | | |
| Operating Profit | $ 60,000 | $ 240,000 | $ 480,000 |
| Interest & Taxes | 6,000 | 48,000 | 120,000 |
| Net Profit (Loss) | $ 54,000 | $ 192,000 | $ 360,000 |

*USI financial projections*

# ACKNOWLEDGING THE COST OF CAPITAL

No matter when you decide to raise capital, you need to be aware of the costs. Funding will have a direct impact on your business vision, value realization, and personal satisfaction. As you examine the various sources of funding, make sure you understand how much equity and control you may be giving away. For debt financing, make sure you understand the cash flow burden created by the loan and the impact on your equity if you cannot service the loan. The financial and control implications of your choice of funding could leave you questioning why you started up in the first place.

When I launched USI, I thought about using outside capital to seed the business. I quickly learned that the cost of startup funding from friends and family outweighed the potential benefits. I also learned that the cost of a business loan in terms of red tape, collateral requirements, and principal and interest payments was just too high.

As a result, I decided to bootstrap. It was one of the best decisions that I ever made. I capitalized USI with $100,000 of my own money. We quickly turned our preorders into a contractual revenue stream, reached breakeven in our fourth month, and never looked back. We used our profits to fund all our growth going forward. I did not have to give up any control and maintained decision-making authority.

## The Cost of Equity—Ownership Control

Not everyone can bootstrap. If you are launching a business that requires a long runway to build out technology, attract a critical mass of users, or develop and test a highly complex product, you will probably need outside funding.

Before you set out to raise money, you should establish decision parameters around all of the following control points:

- Decision-making authority
- Motivation & reward system control
- Work environment autonomy
- Freedom to fulfill business vision
- Value realization and exit strategy flexibility

Since capital is the primary negotiating lever impacting control, you must quantify how much you need and when you need it. And you should consider how many times you may need to go back to your investors for additional funds because each round of financing will reduce your equity and your control.

Before seeking equity financing, think through the following questions to test your comfort level with the possible costs.

- What percentage of ownership will your investors require in return for the funds they invest?
- Will you require multiple rounds of financing to achieve your business vision?
- Will your investors make you change your business plan and vision?
- Will your investors pressure you to grow too quickly and threaten quality control?
- Will your investors require you to pay out a portion of the profits rather than reinvesting your profits in the business?
- Will your investors force you into a premature exit so that they can realize their target return?

While there are downsides to selling equity stakes, you may also find investors who can contribute significant benefits to your startup. Keep in mind that investors can

- Bring a fresh perspective and provide unique advice that can propel your business;

- Provide access to specialized resources, including new management team members;

- Connect you with potential customers and help you land new business;

- Connect you with vendors and help you structure new supplier contracts; and

- Introduce you to a new set of investors for additional financing rounds.

As you meet with potential investors, seek out people who understand you, your motivations, and your goals. Make sure the chemistry is strong with the potential for a long-term relationship built on trust.

## The Importance of Valuation

If you decide to raise equity financing, you will need a clear-cut method for valuing your business. Valuation is the process of determining the worth of your business. Both objective and subjective factors play a role in valuation. In a publicly traded company, current valuation is determined by the stock market—the price of the stock times the total shares outstanding. In a startup, valuation is determined by milestone achievements, strategic fit, potential returns, and negotiation. In fact, valuation of a startup can be more of an art than a science.

Investors typically look at a number of variables, including the following:

- Financial projections
- Product viability
- Contractual preorders
- Working business model
- Clear path to profitability
- Management team
- Competitive differentiation
- Market opportunity
- Intellectual property
- Growth potential

Investors also compare financial metrics, including revenues, earnings, and cash flow, to those of comparable companies. They build models factoring a multiple of revenues and/or EBITDA, discounted cash flow, plus a valuation of existing assets, or a combination to determine value.

The valuation multiple of a particular business is determined by a number of factors, including

- Size of customer base or user community
- Contractual revenues vs. transactional revenues
- Contract terms and duration

- Size of gross, operating, and net margins
- Industry multiples
- Recent comparables

For example, if a standard multiple for a transactional one-off business is five (5) times EBITDA, and current year EBITDA is $5 million, then the business could be valued at $25 million.

Each time a company completes a round of funding, is acquired, or goes public, new valuations and comparables are created. It's up to you to be aware of the valuation activity in your industry and to collect research to back up your estimates of your company's value.

In any event, when you are negotiating to raise money from equity investors, the investors will try to keep the valuation low enough to minimize their financial risk and maximize their control and return on investment. They will want to get as large a piece of your business as possible in return for the money they give you. Naturally, as an entrepreneur, you will want the opposite.

The more you can optimize your valuation, the stronger your position will be during the negotiation. Your objective in the negotiation is to maintain control of your business by building an arsenal of facts to support your position. You can increase your leverage and preparedness by hiring an experienced valuation advisor, transaction attorney, and/or top-quality CPA to work with you before and during negotiations.

## The Cost of Debt—Interest

If you decide that borrowing money is the best way to fund your business, you need to understand the cost of borrowing including interest rates and principal payments. The interest the lender charges is the price you pay in exchange for the use of their money. The rate depends upon six factors: prevailing interest rates, collateral, credit rating, perception of business risk, competition for the loan, and the lender's perception of your character and integrity. Lenders assess your creditworthiness based on their judgment of your ability to make timely payments against the loan. Once you get a loan, making timely payments will have a direct impact on your ability to secure future loans at competitive rates.

A going concern with a solid record of positive cash flow and consistent profits may pay from one point to three points (one point equals one percentage point) over an established benchmark lending rate. Of course, you will pay more as a startup, if you can get the loan.

If your business is already up and running, the lender will want to see documentation that your cash flow can cover the monthly payments. Once the loan is approved, you will be required to sign a lending agreement documenting specific covenants and repayment terms. If you miss a payment, you should expect to pay late fees. If you become delinquent on multiple occasions, the bank will likely exercise their rights to create a direct attachment to your cash flow. For example, if your customers pay you by credit card, the lender can demand that those payments be diverted to cover the loan. The lender can also make a direct attachment to your bank account.

Consider the following questions when seeking a loan:

- Can your cash flow cover the monthly interest payments?

- What are your business assets worth, and can they be used for collateral?

- What action can the lender take against your business or you personally, if you fail to make a payment?

Before you approach lenders, research documentation requirements and prepare the information for your meetings. Keep in mind that your objective is to secure the best terms possible. As part of your preparation, you will need a brief business plan, past and current financials, growth projections, tax returns, and a completed loan application that demonstrates your ability to make the loan payments. You will also need an understanding of your creditworthiness, prevailing interest rates, potential collateral requirements, and a willingness to provide a personal guarantee.

You will gain the most leverage by investing the time to make multiple lenders compete for your business. If possible, work with a trusted advisor, such as your accountant or attorney, to help you secure a loan that is fair and will not put your business in jeopardy.

You will also need a succinct way to explain the viability and value of your business. In other words, you will need a clear and concise pitch.

## DEVELOPING AND DELIVERING YOUR PITCH

In order to engage with investors, you will need a business plan and a presentation, commonly referred to as a pitch deck, covering the basic questions investors and lenders ask. Typically, you need to boil down your business plan into a one- to three-page executive summary. Your pitch should be as succinct as possible—no more than 10 PowerPoint slides—and should convey the highlights of your business.

Your plan and your pitch should include answers to the following questions:

- What problem are you solving (pain point)?

- What is your idea, and how will it solve the problem?

- Who is your target customer?

- What is your business model and how does it work?

- How big is the market opportunity and how is it trending?

- Who are your competitors, and what is your advantage?

- How will you scale your business?

- Who is on your management team, and what do they contribute?

- When will you reach breakeven and become profitable?

- How much money can you make, and how much money do you need?

- What proof points have you achieved?

Investors are looking for a significant return on their investment, and lenders want their entire loan to be paid back on time. You have to persuade your investors and lenders that your management team is uniquely qualified to execute the plan, build the business, and achieve the profit goals.

Even if you decide to bootstrap your business, you should take the time to think through and answer all of the questions investors and lenders ask. As we discussed in *The Startup Roadmap* and in chapter 3, "Dynamic Planning," you will substantially improve your probability of startup success if you have a solid plan before you launch.

## Connecting with Investors

One of the most common ways to connect with potential investors is through a pitching event. Typically, you are given two minutes to make your pitch to a panel of investors. The investors then pepper you with questions for five minutes before moving on to the next presenter. This process was developed to winnow the list of presenters to the best few. The short-listed entrepreneurs are usually given the opportunity to make longer presentations to interested investors as the next step in the process.

# UNDERSTANDING THE INVESTOR'S POINT OF VIEW

Investors are a skeptical lot—and for good reason. Investing in start-ups is a risky proposition. Imagine a constant barrage of requests for money to underwrite ideas that entrepreneurs are convinced will change the world. Given new business failure rates at over 75 percent, investors need to be cautious and judicious with their time and capital.

Since the number of entrepreneurs seeking startup funding is greater than the supply of investors, sometimes investors can come across as cold, calculating, and seemingly dismissive. To first-time entrepreneurs, pitching a professional investor can be intimidating—like making a request of the great and powerful Oz.

Even though investors can be intimidating, they do have money to invest, and they want to invest it to make it grow. But they don't want to lose it and feel foolish. Savvy entrepreneurs know how to minimize the drama by confidently presenting proof points that make the case for investing.

Examples of proof points that can shift the leverage from the investor to the entrepreneur include the following:

- Working prototype

- Contractual preorders

- Customer testimonials

- Working business model

- Existing revenue stream

- Clear path to profitability

- Distinctive competence

- Technological advantage

- Significant market opportunity

- Superior management team

- Proven record of success

If you can demonstrate that you have achieved a majority of these proof points, you will optimize negotiating leverage with qualified investors for the capital you need to grow your business.

## DETERMINING YOUR SOURCE OF FUNDING

Once you have figured out how much funding you need, thoroughly considered the cost of your choice of capital, and developed your pitch, you can investigate the funding options available to you. Funding options include the following:

- Other people's money (OPM)
  - Friends and family—equity or debt
  - Small business loans—bank or SBA
- Your own money—bootstrapping
  - Personal savings
  - Life insurance
  - Home equity
  - Personal loans
  - Credit cards
- Beyond friends, family, and banks
  - Equity investors—angels and venture capitalists (VCs)
  - Alternative funding sources
  - Crowdfunding
  - Convertible debt
  - Additional lending sources
  - Vendor financing
  - Economic development funds
  - Microloans

## OTHER PEOPLE'S MONEY

When I was starting my business, USI, I couldn't wait to lift off. I had decided to leave my corporate career and was impatient to get started as an entrepreneur. But first I had to decide how to fund my startup. As I said in chapter 5, my accountant counseled me to use *other people's money*. I'll never forget his response to my inquiry about startup funding: "OPM, Eddie, OPM."

## Friends and Family—Equity and Debt

Finding outside investors or lenders for a business that is still in the idea stage and has no revenue can be very challenging. That is why the most common route for entrepreneurs seeking OPM is to first approach the people they know best. So I set out to source seed funding from friends and family. But my discussions came to a screeching halt when I realized three things:

- First, I was very concerned about putting my friends' and family's hard-earned money at risk.

- Second, I didn't want to damage the relationships if the business failed.

- Third, I didn't want friends and family telling me how to run the business—especially since they lacked experience in the commercial real estate field.

Entering a round of fund-raising with friends and family can make sense if the people who invest or lend you money have experience with startups. It can also make sense if they have industry knowledge they can contribute to the business, such as high-value connections and/or technical skills. But none of these factors were present as I thought over my list of friends and family.

I would be remiss not to mention that I did secure a small loan from my mother without any strings attached—other than an interest payment that exceeded the CD rate by one percent.

## Business Loans

If you have a long-standing relationship with a bank, you can approach them for a business loan, while recognizing that banks do not normally make loans to startups. If your bank will consider lending you the money, you will be required to complete an extensive loan application, provide a complete set of financials along with a business plan, provide a personal guarantee that the loan will be repaid, and provide collateral for the loan.

## SBA Loans

If you cannot secure a business loan from a local bank, you can try to secure a Small Business Administration (SBA) loan. The SBA doesn't actually make the loan, but the SBA does provide a guarantee for the loan if the borrower passes the SBA screening process with an accredited SBA lender.

The SBA does not require fully collateralized loans, as they are willing to take some risk and bet on the promise of the business. Even so, the SBA lender will want to understand the business model, the financial projections, and the economic conditions affecting the business.

## Line of Credit

If you decide that you want to pursue other forms of business borrowing, you can attempt to establish a line of credit with a bank. A line of credit gives you access to a preapproved amount of borrowing at a variable interest rate. One of the features of a line of credit is that you can draw on and repay the loan on a flexible basis, only paying interest on the amount outstanding until the principal is due.

A line of credit can build your business's credit rating, get you over rough spots, and provide short-term funding for operations (working capital). Setting up a line of credit is smart, but you need to be aware that a line of credit is structured to be repaid on an annual basis. If your business can generate a greater return with the borrowed money than the interest rate you are paying to use it, then tapping a line of credit probably makes sense.

## Using Your Own Money—Bootstrapping

As I said earlier, when launching my business, I realized that bootstrapping was my best pathway. As the sole funder, I could maintain ownership control and answer only to myself. I would use my savings as startup capital and forego a salary for the first year. Then, I would bootstrap USI's growth by reinvesting all of the business's income.

Deciding to bootstrap is a big step. There are real trade-offs and opportunity costs to consider.

- Do you have the personal resources to invest in your business without betting the ranch?

- Are you comfortable with putting your own money at risk to fund a brand new enterprise with an unknown outcome?

- Can you accept the fact that the money you invest in your business will no longer be available for personal contingencies or to buy a car, fund education, buy a home, or save for retirement?

- What if the business fails? Can you withstand such an outcome?

When you use your own money, fear of failure becomes your greatest motivator. Besides the business obligations, I had a family with two children under five to support. I had to succeed because there was no Plan B. I was going to do everything I could to ensure that my business would prosper.

If you decide to bootstrap, you can secure capital to fund your startup from the following personal sources:

- Personal savings
- The cash value of a whole life insurance policy
- A home equity loan
- A personal loan
- Credit cards—but only as a last resort

### Savings

Personal savings are the cheapest source of startup funding. Although you lose the opportunity to invest the cash elsewhere, there is no direct cost for using these funds. Beyond liquid savings, including stocks and bonds, your 401(k) or retirement savings are also sources of funds, but they do have restrictions that need to be considered. Utilizing personal savings enables you to maximize control, but at the same time it forces you to shoulder the lion's share of the risk.

### Whole Life Insurance Loan

If you do not have liquid savings, a whole life policy is the next least expensive source of funds. The cash value is liquid, and you can take it out any time for any reason. With a life insurance loan, you borrow against the cash value in your policy, typically up to 90 percent of the surrender value. The interest rate you pay on the loan will be only slightly above the policy's internal rate of return.

## *Home Equity Loan*

Using your home as collateral will minimize your borrowing costs. However, you will need to demonstrate home equity value above the existing mortgage debt. Of course, the best time to borrow is during a low-interest rate environment. When your potential returns are above the cost of capital, using leverage is an intelligent choice.

## *Personal Loan*

If you are seeking a personal loan as a source of funds, you should expect to pay a higher interest rate than a mortgage rate. The bank will require the loan to be collateralized by other personal assets, such as your savings. Personal loans can be structured as either a line of credit or as a term loan. A term loan is for a specific amount, at a fixed rate of interest, repaid evenly over a set term.

## *Credit Cards (Not Recommended)*

The most expensive and most risky way to fund your startup is with credit card debt. Since a startup can burn through capital at a significant rate, and credit card interest rates are so dangerously high, funding your startup with a credit card can bury you in personal debt that can take years to pay off. Be advised that the issuer may offer a teaser rate to start, but inevitably, the rate will rise dramatically. Read the fine print on your credit card agreement. Credit cards should only be used as a bridge or as a last resort.

## How I Bootstrapped

My wife and I had been saving up to purchase a house. After months of debating the startup and funding decisions, we finally agreed to make the sacrifice and shift our priorities from buying a house to investing our savings in the business.

Once I made the decision to bootstrap, I never looked back. I did not have to struggle with the monthly cash drain of repaying a loan. I didn't have to worry about losing my relatives' or friends' money. But most importantly, I did not have equity investors looking over my shoulder, second-guessing my business decisions. I had complete control over who I hired and where and how I operated. Having control over business strategy and decision-making increased productivity, streamlined operations, and maximized my personal satisfaction. In the long run, bootstrapping enabled USI to enjoy rapid growth, as we kept plowing the profits back into the business.

If you are willing to take the risk, bootstrapping can be a powerful way to fund your startup and maintain control.

# MOVING BEYOND FRIENDS, FAMILY, AND BANKS

## Equity Investors—Angels and VCs

Professional equity investors, such as angels and venture capitalists, provide funding to entrepreneurs, usually in exchange for an ownership stake in your new business venture. They are usually sophisticated investors with access to capital, industry expertise, and substantial relationship networks that can enable a business to flourish. At the same time, their goal is to maximize their returns on their investments by getting as large an ownership share as possible in exchange for their funding.

If you are raising equity financing from professional investors at the seed stage, you will be asked to give away a bigger portion of your company than you would at a later stage. Investors prefer companies that have proven they can generate revenue or—even better—a profit. The more you can grow your business first by bootstrapping, the better deal you can negotiate when you seek an outside investor.

Many investors, particularly angels, will invest as a group. If you are trying to raise a large amount of money (over $1 million), then they will release portions of the funds to you in what are called tranches. You will have to meet certain milestones, performance thresholds, and benchmarks to trigger the release of each tranche.

While the media is full of stories about venture capitalists investing in startups, the truth is that VCs seldom actually do. Typically, their role comes at a later stage. It is angel investors that usually provide funding at the seed stage. However, angels typically invest after the owner has put his or her own capital at risk.

Angels and private investors receive hundreds of business plans and pitches on a regular basis. On average, angels fund two and a half percent of startups they review. VCs fund less than one percent.

Before you approach any professional investor, do your homework. Find out how they invest and what they like to invest in. Most angels and VCs invest in what they know—in their area of distinctive competence. Professional investors target their investments to certain stages of development (seed, early stage, and growth).

If you are going to pursue an equity investor relationship for startup funding, you should invest the time to get to know the angel funding community before you make your pitch. Attending investor forums, conducting informational interviews, and networking with professional investors will build your knowledge, your confidence, and your understanding of investment criteria.

### *The 7-Step Angel Funding Process*

As an angel investor, I use the following 7-step process for making investment decisions. The 7-Step Angel Funding Process enables the entrepreneur and the angel to complete a deep dive into the entrepreneur's vision and business model. This enables both the entrepreneur and the angel to jointly assess the genuine potential for working together.

The three-hour agenda for the 7-Step Angel Funding Process is outlined below:

### Step 1: Brief Introductions—10 Minutes

### Step 2: Business Idea—20 Minutes

- How did you come up with the idea?
- Describe your product and the pain it resolves.
- Who is your ideal customer?
- What is the size of the market?
- Who is your competition?
- Quantify the business opportunity.

### Step 3: Value Proposition—30 Minutes

- How does your product work?
- What is your value proposition?
- Is your value proposition compelling? Why?
- How does your product help your customer succeed?
- Does your customer believe that it helps them succeed?

### Step 4: Customer Demand—15 Minutes

- Do you have any customers?
- Who was your first paying customer, and why did they buy?
- How many paying customers do you have?
- How do you measure customer demand?

### Step 5: Business Model—45 Minutes

- How do you make money?
- What are your sources of revenue?
- What are your primary expenses?
- How much have you already invested/spent? Please quantify.
- How long will it take to reach breakeven?
- Present your current financials.

### Step 6: Realistic Discussion and Strategy for the Way Forward—30 Minutes

- How do you value your business?
- How much money do you really need to achieve breakeven?
- What is your ideal form of funding—debt or equity?
- Generate a timeline of accomplishments & challenges.
- What are your top three obstacles?
- Can you partner with a customer, supplier, or competitor to better realize your business vision?

## Step 7: Tough Questions—30 Minutes

- What are your management team's qualifications?
- Can you implement the plan?
- Are you being realistic?
- Do you have the stomach for it?
- Are you willing to make the sacrifice?
- Is it worth the risk?
- When will you make a profit?
- What are your next steps?

To complete the 7-Step Angel Investment Process, the entrepreneur needs to prepare a slide deck with financial projections and support materials.

One of the reasons I have written *The Purpose Is Profit* is to help filter angel funding requests. I believe it is important for the entrepreneur to know how an angel investor thinks.

## Alternative Funding Sources

### *Crowdfunding*

Crowdfunding is an Internet-based, capital-raising vehicle created to enable anyone to seek financing for projects and new ventures. Unlike raising money from angels and venture capitalists, the amount of capital that you can raise is limited only by the number of consumers interested in your venture and the size of their wallets. In addition, crowdfunding enables you to keep control of your business, as you don't need to sell equity in order to raise capital.

If you are interested in raising capital on the Internet, you can present your new business idea and funding requirements to consumers on a crowdfunding site. Interested consumers—more commonly referred to as supporters—commit capital, enabling your venture to lift off. You need to recognize their participation by sending them an acknowledgement, typically in the form of a product or accessory. If you plan on crowdfunding, you should make a video to explain your product and state your case to funders. You should also promote your campaign through social media and your own personal network, lining up supporters before you launch your effort. Before engaging a crowdfunding program, you should study other successful campaigns to learn what works.

At some crowdfunding sites, if you don't succeed in meeting your fund-raising goal, you may not be able to collect the amount already pledged to your project—but you may still have to pay the fee to the site. Also, you may have difficulty protecting your intellectual property once you've put your idea on the Internet. So set your goals carefully before using this form of funding.

On the positive side, using crowdfunding can raise your profile and give you exposure to lots of potential new customers. Many entrepreneurs view crowdfunding as a form of marketing. It is a very good way to line up preorders, leads, and early buzz for your product.

### *Equity Crowdfunding*

The Jumpstart Our Business Startups Act (JOBS Act), passed in 2012, is designed to take crowdfunding to a new level. The idea is to democratize small business investments to stimulate the economy. The JOBS Act has legalized equity crowdfunding and removed some of the regulatory hurdles for unaccredited investors to invest in startups for profit. "Equity crowdfunding" means that your company will actually issue shares of stock to the people who pledge funds. At equity crowdfunding sites, supporters are investing in your company, not just your idea or project, and will, in effect, become your business partners if the offering is successful.

If you are thinking of using equity crowdfunding to raise capital, you should become familiar with the details of the JOBS Act and the associated SEC regulations.

### Convertible Debt

An alternative funding mechanism for startups is the convertible note, which essentially starts out as a short-term loan at the seed stage. The security is convertible into equity (usually in the form of preferred stock) at the investor's option when the security matures, and is convertible into equity at the company's option when the entrepreneur closes the next round of financing.

The convertible note has become popular because holders of debt do not receive any portion of the company's equity prior to conversion. That means the founding entrepreneurs do not have to set a valuation for their company or dilute their equity in the company until a later stage. However, establishing the conversion ratio (the number of shares of stock each investor will receive upon converting the outstanding principal of the note) may require at least an informal valuation.

Entrepreneurs who pursue convertible debt financing believe their business valuation will improve as they grow and would prefer to let the next stage of financing set the valuation. At the same time, investors in convertible debt can "hedge their bets" on a startup company: If the company fails, they have seniority to reclaim available assets before stockholders get a penny. If the company succeeds, they can convert their securities into equity and participate in future growth.

Convertible debt can be risky for startups, as it may be difficult to attract additional capital with debt of any kind (even convertible debt) on your books. Also, the legal and accounting fees for an offering of convertible debt may be equivalent to those of an offering of common or preferred stock. The deals can get complex with the setting of interest rates, the maturity date for the note, the conversion ratio, and the imposition of caps on the stock price. If the company hasn't yet reached its milestones and is not ready for the next round of funding by the maturity date of the security, the company will be required to make an immediate cash payment of principal and accrued interest to each investor. If the company does not have enough cash to make this payment, the investors will lose some portion of their principal, and the company will likely go out of business.

This is a complicated form of financing suited to high-growth ventures with substantial capital requirements. Anyone seeking to structure a convertible debt deal at the seed stage needs to hire a qualified attorney steeped in venture funding and convertible debt experience. Thoughtful drafting of the terms and conditions within the convertible debt contract enables the entrepreneur and the investor to minimize risk.

## Additional Lending Sources

### Vendor Financing

As long as the interest rates are competitive, vendor financing is a reasonable way to fund a startup. One of my angel investments, Infinity Fitness, secured financing from the manufacturer of their exercise equipment. This financing provided cash-flow relief during the launch phase. Likewise, tech startups can often strike a deal with designers or coders to take payment in equity rather than cash. In such cases, the vendor becomes a part owner of the company with a vested interest in its success.

## Economic Development Funds

States and municipalities may make loans and occasional grants to businesses in special economic development zones. When dealing with economic development funds, you will need to make a case that your business will create jobs and contribute to the local economy. You will also have to present financial statements and a business plan. In some states, the borrower must attend classes in finance and business to be eligible for a loan. Most economic development departments offer technical assistance to small business owners who wish to take advantage of their programs. Grants are often restricted to industries the government agency wants to develop, such as green energy, biotechnology, or high-tech manufacturing.

## Microloans

Entrepreneurs who do not qualify for a traditional loan and are typically in a lower income bracket may apply for a microloan of $25,000 to $50,000 in certain jurisdictions. The SBA provides the funds to local nonprofit intermediaries, who in turn lend the money with their own repayment terms. Some funds aim to help minority- or women-owned businesses. Typically, the funds can be used for working capital, raw materials, furniture, repairs, equipment, or machinery.

## MAKING THE RIGHT FUNDING DECISION

Like you, I made the decision to become an entrepreneur. I wanted to take control and build my own business. I wanted to create genuine value for my customers, make the decisions, and be accountable for the outcomes. I knew my choice of funding was crucial to my objective of maintaining control.

Every entrepreneur wrestles with the need for startup funding. How do you determine how much capital you really need? What are the essentials of financial modeling and forecasting? What are the costs of capital—both equity and debt? How does valuation influence cost and control? What are the sources of funding—friends and family, bootstrapping, angels and VCs, or alternative sources?

Since I could not secure outside funding under the terms and timing I needed, I decided to take the brunt of the risk and bootstrap. I invested $100,000 of my own money. At the time, it seemed like a monumental risk, but very quickly, I started landing customers and contracts. We achieved profitability in our fourth month, used our earnings to build the business, maintained control, and never needed outside funding.

As you pursue funding alternatives, you need to be very thoughtful about the future value of your equity. In the moment, you can trade off a lifetime of value for a relatively small sum of money.

Remember that your funding decision will have a direct impact on your business vision, value realization, and ultimately, your personal satisfaction.

# ACKNOWLEDGMENTS

In many respects, writing a book is the equivalent of starting a new business. *The Purpose Is Profit* was no exception. Like every successful new business, in addition to planning, funding, creating, and marketing, we needed a powerful and dedicated support team. These are the people that challenged us every step of the way to build a better mousetrap.

## ED'S FAMILY

Since my wife, Barbara, was a direct participant in my entrepreneurial journey, her perspective and insight played an invaluable role in helping document the story in this book. Besides being my life partner and my financial partner, Barbara was the company's first financial officer—and a very good one at that. Without her contributions and loving support, this book would not have come to fruition.

After traveling the world with me on a global consulting assignment, my son Paul agreed to join us in developing *The Purpose Is Profit*. Through his writing and editing, Paul helped to bring the millennial voice to this book. My elder son, James, contributed ground-level perspective as an aspiring entrepreneur while working at General Assembly, one of New York's high-growth startups. Finally, my daughter, Frances, provided the engineering viewpoint as a blog writer while working toward her chemical engineering degree at Vanderbilt. I am very grateful for all of their contributions and for having the honor of working with them.

## WYN'S FAMILY

I am eternally grateful to my husband, John, not only for his steadfast support over my years of working with entrepreneurs, but especially for his critical eye, keen insights, and objective perspective as Ed and I labored to create this book. His contributions helped make our product one that I hope will truly benefit aspiring entrepreneurs for years to come.

My daughter, Drew, and my son, Bob, each encouraged me, acted as sounding boards, raised perceptive questions and comments, and enthusiastically shared excerpts from our book with their entrepreneurial friends. Thank you, Drew and Bob. I will always appreciate all you have done.

## OUR TEAM

Mary Jo Krump has tirelessly fulfilled the role of social media director—a tall order with the ever-expanding media platforms needed to reach our global market. Mary Jo helped edit our book, crafted our advertising campaigns, implemented our content marketing programs, managed our contact database, strengthened our follower engagement, and persevered in building *The Purpose Is Profit* brand.

Brian Bellew has been a devoted friend, advisor, and editor of this book. As an early member of the USI team, Brian had firsthand knowledge and insight into the history and evolution of the company. Brian's command of the English language, combined with his precision editing, had a material impact on *The Purpose Is Profit*.

As an intern, Rebecca Lovering helped create a solid foundation for the growth of our social media, content marketing, and database management. When Rebecca departed for graduate school, Omar Douglass joined the team as a writer, editor, and blogger. Omar challenged the status quo and gave our blogs on entrepreneurship and startups a fresh voice.

My sister, Kathryn McLaughlin, has always looked after her brother as supporter, friend, and legal advisor. As my attorney, Kathy represented USI's legal interests and provided guidance on intellectual property law for *The Purpose Is Profit*.

We were fortunate to secure critical feedback on early drafts and individual chapters from Rick Krump and Brian Krump. They provided technical insights and recommendations to improve the precision of our writing while encouraging us to educate through story. My cousin Mark McLaughlin and his wife, Carol Ann, benchmarked our content against their own entrepreneurial experience while providing consistent moral support throughout the life of the project. Finally, my brothers-in-law, Charlie Boyd and Harvey Smith, and my sister-in-law, Amy Smith, provided encouragement, support, and recommendations that strengthened our content.

Every worthy endeavor relies on both internal and external resources to come to successful completion. We had the good fortune to work with a number of talented professionals from Greenleaf Book Group and Smith Publicity. Production manager Tyler LeBleu was the quarterback from Greenleaf who took us across the goal line. Tyler was supported by a host of Greenleaf professionals, including art director Neil Gonzalez, senior editor Nathan True, copy editor Sally Garland, and project manager Emilie Lyons. The lead contact for our public relations campaign was Corinne Moulder, with Kristi Hughes as the project publicist from Smith Publicity.

We would be remiss not to mention the early contributions and kindness of Pat Scully. Before engaging in our relationship with Greenleaf, we worked with Pat Scully Design. Pat took the time as an independent contractor to educate us on the details of book design. She used her significant talents to design the PreRelease Snapshot of *The Purpose Is Profit* and the first publication of *The Startup Roadmap*.

Finally, we would like to acknowledge the ongoing encouragement and support provided by Roseann Fitzgerald, my classmate from the College of the Holy Cross. In many respects, writing a book is like going down a very long, dark tunnel, striving for the light. Roseann was a beacon, offering kind words of support and facilitating connections throughout our journey.

## THE INNER CIRCLE

During the early days of writing *The Purpose Is Profit*, a three-year endeavor, we cultivated global relationships with an important group of contributors from diverse backgrounds and professional aspirations. We refer to this special group as our Inner Circle. They invested the time to provide preliminary feedback on early sample material to improve *The Purpose Is Profit*. They encouraged us with their comments, shared their expertise, and helped form the foundation for a much larger following. In recognition of their early contributions and encouragement, we want to call out our Inner Circle Members by name below.

## Inner Circle Members

Vlad Alexandrescu

Stephanie Anderson

Eduardo Anunciação

Mallory Arents

Alan Arnett

Milton Ayala

Gregory D. Baekey, CLU, ChFC

Hector Bassett

Catherine Beckmann

Mark Birch

George Bradt

Wayne Breitbarth

Stephen Brooks

Ivette K. Caballero

Lloyd Cambridge

Fred Campbell

Stefania Chandelier

Alicia Chasse

Fazley Shabab Chowdhury

Justin Christopher

Guy Cleveland

Isaiah Cooper

Robert Coursen

Daniella Cracknell

Susana de Sola

Tekaligne "TK" Debre

Mike Denton

Gustavo Dias

Michael Dolce

Odet L. Douglass

Orion Douglass

Shirley A. Douglass

Spiros Drakatos

John Drummey, CFA

David du Plessis

Michael Eagleton

Steve Ehrlich

Cliff Ennico

Paul Ferraro

Jeff Fortin

Alyssa Fricke

Brian Froelich

Hon. Count David J. Gagnon, D.D., Ph.D., FWCI

Craig Gambardella

Inge Geerdens

Helmuth A. Geiser

Fodil Ghezzal

Andy Goldstrom

Dustin Goodpaster

Don Gordon

Jason Greene

Jørgen Grøndal

Mike Harris

Stephanie Hayden

Andrew Hayes

Henriette Hedløv

Hon. Tamer Hegazy

Chris Hollis

Michelle Hutchinson

Stelios Ioannou

Shreekrishna Joshi

Fambo S. Kakinga

Tim Kane

John Karamanos

Harold L. Kestenbaum

Lauren Keyson

John Kluge

James Peter Krasnow

Robbie Kunkel

Martin Lightsey

Teresa LoPorto

Andrew Markwell B.App. Sc.(Hons)

Mariona Borras Mata

Monica Matthews

Bob McCracken

Michael "Mike" R. McLane

Adèle McLay

Joe McMullen

Arline Melzer

Harry A. Metzger III

Abhishek Mishra

Eric Mockler

John Nagella

Robert Newell

Ray Noble

Sergi Nogues

Brett Noyes

Augustina Tessy Nwachukwuoji

Kevin O'Neill

Christina Otto

Paula M. Parker

Diane Paterson

Debra Pimentel

Leonard Pimentel

Art Pozner

Pablo Prahl

Michael Quinlan

Mary Donahue Quinlan

Brendan Rafalski

Prajakt Raut

Larry Reilly

Sarah L. Robinson

Ron Rosener

Lisa Rothstein

Felicia Rubinstein

Jay Rutherford

Malcolm Ryder

Stefano Sanchini

Prof. Arun Sangwan (FIIB)

Evangeline Sawad

Kinshuk Saxena

A. Scher

Fred Schmidt

Kate Schwid

John Seniszyn

Zack Shariff

Nancy Sheed

Dr. S. Vincent Shin

Haakon Skar

Kraighton Stack

Jeff Stoltman

Anoop Sud

Ingrid Tappin

Dan Tefft

Vanessa Thompson

Pam Timbes

Patrick Tinney

Michael Toebe

Luis Trillo

Abhishek Tripathi

Victor Tuohy

Ken Wagner

Joe Wasylyk

Matthew Weiner

Lanny White

Jari Wirzenius

Subrina Wood

# INDEX

angel investors, 283–284
benefits from investors, 269
business valuation and, 269–271
control points, 268
costs of, 267–268
family and friends, 74–76, 81, 278
private equity firms, 162, 172,
175–176
venture capitalists, 283–284
ethics, 11, 163–165
execution
operating plans, 44
resource requirements, 241–242
exit scenarios, 50
expansion. *See* growth
expenses, 49, 260
cash expenditures for assets, 263–264
cost of revenues (goods sold), 260
cost-reduction goals, 198
direct costs, 246, 247, 248
financial discipline, 154–155
indirect, 246
minimizing, 34, 161–162
monthly burn rate, 250
office space, 73
overhead, 48, 156, 244, 247, 261
personal sacrifice, 80–81
personnel costs, 44, 73, 163, 202
pre-startup, 37
in profit validation, 243–244
projected costs, 73, 152–153
service delivery, 46, 90, 220
experience, 12, 21, 23, 25, 104, 218
expertise, 28, 117, 219, 251. *See also*
distinctive competence

## F

facilities management, 173, 180
failure

fear of, 81, 215, 280
learning from, 117–118
points of, 115–116
family
equity sharing, 74–76, 81, 278
loans from, 76, 81, 278
personal sacrifice, 80–81
FDA, 11
fears, 1, 9, 81, 215, 280
fees
for late payments, 272
legal, 10, 165, 290
revenue from, 43, 44, 45, 72, 231
Field, Annette, 14
field execution, 44
finances. *See also* cash flow; expenses;
revenue
assets, 263–264
balance sheets, 265
calculations, 246–250
discipline, 154–155
models, 48–49, 72, 154, 259
projections, 243, 244, 245–249,
265–266
statements, 185, 265
valuation of business, 269–271, 289
financing. *See* funding; loans
flexibility, 51, 181, 189–190
founders' equity, 73
friends
equity sharing, 74–76, 81, 278
loans from, 76, 81, 278
Froude, Don, 10, 63
funding
angel-funding process, 285–287
bootstrapping, 79, 81, 108, 280–283
convertible debt, 289–290
costs associated with, 71, 73, 79, 154,
267–273

innovation, 12, 23, 125, 181
integrity, 11, 20, 163–165
intellectual property, 31, 62, 66, 288
interest rates, 77, 104, 271–272, 282
Internet
  dot-com businesses, 145–146
  marketing platforms, 65–66, 67, 238,
    288
  raising capital on, 287–288
inventory, 116, 263–264
investment bankers
  finding, 173–174
  role in offering memorandums,
    184–185
  selecting, 174
investors, 73–74, 171. *See also* funding
  benefits from, 269
  business valuation and, 270
  connecting with, 275
  friends and family as, 74–76, 278
  to fund acquisitions, 173–174
  ownership control, 75, 268
  point of view, 275–276
  presenting financial model to, 258
  return on investment, 274

**J**

Johnson, Henry, 16, 99
Johnson Controls (JCI)
  about company, 181, 191–192
  acquisition of USI, 181–182, 183,
    187–189
  acquisition of York International,
    195–197
  decision to leave company, 207
  human resources at, 200–201, 203
  integration of USI into, 194–195,
    198
  management style, 195, 197

Jumpstart Our Business Startups Act
  (JOBS Act), 288, 289

**K**

knowledge, 11, 12, 24

**L**

launch, 83
  addressing unknowns beforehand,
    37, 38
  commitment to, 15
  lining up paying customers prior to,
    105, 152
  of Sigma Communications, 103
  timing of, 50, 151–154
lawyers. *See* attorneys
leadership, 96–97
learning curve, 110
legacy systems, 181
legal business structures, 49–51
legal fees, 10, 165, 290
legal forms, 30
lenders. *See* loans
Level, Lee, 179, 181
leverage
  creation, 186–189
  with investors, 276
  in securing loans, 273
  using to grow business, 74
liability, 30, 50
life insurance loan, 281
listening
  to advisors, 109
  to customers, 41–42, 99
LLC corporations, 50
loans
  bank, 76–77, 278–279
  collateral, 77, 78, 272

growth, 166, 173, 178
line of business management, 98–99,
     202
logo development, 63–64
market valuation, 177
naming, 59–61
product line expansion, 97–99
relationship to Sigma, 113–114
revenue model, 45
secret sauce, 181–182, 192, 194
strategic leadership, 96–97
strategic plans, 189
value proposition, 41
values, 38–39
vision, 38–39
unknowns
addressing prior to launch, 37, 38
outcomes, 79, 280
in sales process, 139

**V**

validation
data for potential buyers, 186
profit, 243–244
proof of concept, 26–28, 104–105
of value proposition, 128–129
valuation, 269–271, 289
value
creation, 20, 140, 150
of flexibility, 189–190
optimization, 187–189
realizing, 190
Value-Managed Relationships, 18
value propositions, 223–224
benefits qualification, 40, 225
benefits quantification, 40, 224
branding and, 58
competitive advantage and, 225
definition, 39

formulation, 128–129, 149–150
marketing plan and, 237–239
of Sigma Communications Inc.,
     105–107
testing strength of, 150–151
USI's, 41, 151
values
defining, 38–39
shared, 195
vendor financing, 290–291
venture capitalists, 74, 283–284
vision
alignment with, 36
branding and, 56
creation, 38–39, 150
realizing, 9

**W**

websites, 65, 66, 237
Westley, Nick, 99–100, 157
work ethic, 32

**Y**

York International, 196–197

# ABOUT THE AUTHORS

## ED "SKIP" MCLAUGHLIN

 Ed is the founder of four businesses and is currently running Blue Sunsets LLC, a real estate and angel investment firm. He bootstrapped his first business, United Systems Integrators (USI) Corporation, a corporate real estate outsourcing firm, and grew it into an Inc. 500 company. In 2001, Ed earned Entrepreneur of the Year honors from Ernst & Young. In 2005, he sold USI to Johnson Controls, a Fortune 100 company, and at that point, became CEO of JCI's Global Workplace Business for the Americas. A member of the Board of Governors for Tufts Medical Center, Ed founded its David E. Wazer Breast Cancer Research Fund. He graduated from the College of the Holy Cross, where he is a member of the Board of Trustees. Active in philanthropy, Ed lives with his wife in Connecticut and has three adult children.

*Email:* Ed@ThePurposeIsProfit.com
*LinkedIn:* www.LinkedIn.com/in/EdSkipMcLaughlin
*Twitter:* @purposeisprofit

*Photo credit: Patrick Broderick Photography*

# WYN LYDECKER

Wyn is the founder of Upstart Business Planning, where she works with entrepreneurs to develop plans that answer the questions investors ask most often. Previously, she was Managing Director of Business Plans International in New York and Co-Director of the Small Business Resource Center at Norwalk Community College. Wyn has an MBA in finance and marketing from the Wharton School of the University of Pennsylvania and a BA in economics from the University of California at Santa Barbara. She serves on the board of a local nonprofit she helped found, At Home In Darien. She lives in Connecticut with her husband and has two adult children.

*Email:* Wyn@ThePurposeIsProfit.com
*LinkedIn:* www.LinkedIn.com/in/WynLydecker
*Photo credit: Cynthia McIntyre Photography*

# PAUL MCLAUGHLIN

Paul is an associate with Deloitte in the Financial Advisory Services Group in the Real Estate Consulting Practice. Previously, Paul served as vice president of Blue Sunsets LLC, where he was responsible for real estate projects and specific angel investments. He has a BA in mathematics from the College of the Holy Cross and an MBA from Georgetown's McDonough School of Business.

*Email:* Paul@ThePurposeIsProfit.com
*LinkedIn:* www.LinkedIn.com/in/PaulPMcLaughlin
*Photo credit: Patrick Broderick Photography*